One Man's Motorcycles

1939-1949

By
Peter McManus

Second Edition

With good wishes

Peter McManus.

**One Man's Motorcycles
1939-1949**

By

Peter McManus

A catalogue record for this book is available from the British Library.

ISBN 0 9530603 2 2

Cover Design: Tranters

Published by M.E.P. Publishers

Printed by Tranters, Markeaton Printing Works
Payne Street, Derby, DE22 3AX
Telephone: 01332 341982

Getting started

Arthur Battelle and I were fellow motorcyclists when we were in our twenties. Arthur was eventually to write a trilogy of books describing his eventful life as an agricultural engineer and authority on tractors, ancient and modern. Meeting him again many years later prompted me to write this book.

So my thanks to Arthur for kick starting me into action, to brother Brian for the Rhyl pictures, to my son Ross and daughter-in-law Stephanie for their invaluable help and, of course, to the entire *dramatis personae* in the book........Not forgetting the motorcycles.

About This Book

Boyhood in Rhyl during the nineteen thirties followed by an engineering apprenticeship in Dickensian conditions in Derby during the War. Rolls Royce aero engine development next, then starting in the motorcycle business after the War.

Buying, selling, restoring, riding and racing motorcycles of the nineteen twenties, thirties and forties.

A motorcycle theme then? Yes, but there's a lot more to it then that. My objective has been to convey the spirit of the times.

It is not a technical book but is written to appeal to the general reader with enough information for him not to just put it back on the shelf but to refer to it time and time again.

It may well be that you are already an aficionado but, if not, you will see that it has been written with tremendous enthusiasm and I hope that some of that enthusiasm will rub off on you.

I first rode a motorcycle in 1939, sixty years ago and since then I have never stopped. During that time motorcycles have given me an enormous amount of pleasure and continue to do so.
So here's to motorcyclists everywhere, past, present and future. Whether your choice is a modern monster or a twenties tiddler you will equally experience the joy of swinging your iron steed round those challenging bends.
Good luck and safe riding from your fellow enthusiast.

Peter McManus

THE ONE MAN'S TRILOGY

One Man's Motorcycles 1939-1949 was the first of Peter McManus' One Man's trilogy. Next came *One Man's Scotland,* a much bigger book with 400 pages and 270 illustrations, many in colour. There are about 50 photographs by the great Lea MacNally, author, stalker, authority on the Red Deer and the Golden Eagle and an award winning wildlife photographer.

The book records Peter's 40 years and more of Highland stalking and the tremendous characters who made stalking history during the last two hundred years. Once again a lighthearted look at the whole scene with short chapters, many illustrations and a diversity of interests. £16.95 softback. Numbered limited edition hardback £29.95.

One Man's Gun Quest completed Peter's One Man's trilogy. Hardback, 250 pages, 240 illustrations, £24.95. Looking back over 50 years of gun collecting made Peter realise that the collectors, shooters and gunsmiths were every bit as interesting as the guns themselves so it is not merely a gun book but a people book.

The illustrations are vital to the book. Excellent photographs, many in colour, by Derbyshire's talented photographer and gun enthusiast, Ernest A. Drury Smith, (Ernie to you and I). Colour photographs lent by the Birmingham gun trade of the most superlative gun engraving. Once again a lighthearted look at the whole scene.

Both books had the benefit of excellent reviews, they sold well and continue to do so. One young Highland stalker sold over 100 copies of the Scottish book.

All books are available signed and post free UK, £2.50 extra Europe, £5 extra rest of the world from M.E.P. Publishers, Newton Park Farm, Newton Solney, Burton on Trent, DE15 0SS Tel. 01283 703280.

NOTES ON THE SECOND EDITION OF ONE MAN'S MOTORCYCLES 1939-1949

The first edition was published in 1999 and went on to be the best selling book in its category, autobiography, at the National Motorcycle Museum. Titch Alien, founder of the Vintage Motorcycle Club, was delighted with it and letters of appreciation flowed in from all over the world.

Out of print for a number of years now despite many requests for a copy but with the forthcoming sale of my motorcycle collection on July 1st 2007 it must be re-published.

This second edition is a copy of the first so there are a number of points that I would like to bring to your attention.

The moving finger writes and having writ moves on and there's not a damn thing that anyone can do about it, as Omar Khyam might have written! So the events recorded up to 1949 obviously cannot be changed!

The first edition, however, was written in 1999 so any contemporary values quoted were those of 1999, not 2007. For example on pages 54/55. We all thought that inflation was bad enough then, but look at. it now!

There are also a few errors that crept in: on page 238 the wartime Moto Guzzi is listed as having the usual inlet over exhaust valve configuration. Unusually, however, in this case it was exhaust over inlet. On page 185 a post war 350cc AJS is illustrated, identical to a Matchless but with a forward facing magneto. Both were made by Associated Motorcycles. The caption should read AJS, not Matchless. The advanced Ascot Pullin on page 144 was designed by Cyril Pullin.

One or two spelling corrections: The speedway rider Freddie Strekker's name should be spelt Strecker. George Pagett of McEvoy fame should be Patchett and finally Tich Allen should be Titch.

CURRENT PROJECT

In early 1917 war in the air intensified on the Western Front in France. No.40 fighter squadron was in the thick of it facing Richthofen's deadly Jagstaffel 11.

Flying in 40 Squadron was Lionel Blaxland and a newcomer was "Mick' Mannock. Mannock got off to a very slow start but the more experienced Lionel Blaxland did his best to keep up Mannock's spirits.

Mannock went on to become the highest scoring British pilot of the war with 73 victories.

Lionel Blaxland's nephew was John Simpkinson of Etwall, Derbyshire, and when he died he left his five photograph albums of those days together with his Flying Log Book to John. Strictly speaking it was forbidden to photograph the plane and pilots in wartime but Lionel had taken no notice and snapped away! The Flying Log Book records every flight he made during the war *on the day.*

Brought up on Biggles I have always been interested in World War One aviation and John has been kind enough to lend it all to me to write the story of Lionel Blaxland and his fellow pilots, including Mannock. None of this has ever been published before.

In addition to this John Batchelor the incomparable aviation artist whose work, in my opinion, is unsurpassed, has very kindly allowed me to use some of his superb illustrations of World War One aircraft for my book.

Lionel Blaxland was a master at Repton for many years until he eventually became the Vicar of Doveridge, Derbyshire, where I had the opportunity to meet him and ply him with questions about those incredible days. So many questions! What kind of man was Mick Mannock? What was it like to fly the Nieuport 17?....and much more! The notes I made at the time have been invaluable in writing the book.

The title of the book is *Richthofen Jagstaffel Ahead* and will be published later this year.

After its publication I hope to write my next book on motorcycles with my account of the years 1950-1980.

Contents

(Top) Peter McManus riding his 1938 350cc Tiger 80 Triumph at a Midlands
grasstrack meeting in 1948.
(Bottom) Harry "T" Tunaley riding his 1949 500cc Triumph Trophy wins his heat in
tremendous style at Cadwell Park racing circuit in 1949.

"Time present and time past
Are both perhaps present in time future
And time future contained in time past"

T.S.Eliot.

Chapter One
Motorcycle Magic

"Motorcycles? Magical? Surely they are noisy, dirty, dangerous things ... and so dreadfully plebeian". This, without doubt, is how Lady Bracknell would have described them: The magic would have completely eluded her. (Lady Bracknell is the overbearing aristocrat in "The Importance of Being Earnest.")

But, make no mistake about it, they ARE magical and once you have been bitten by the motorcycle bug you are never immune again. "Once a motorcyclist, always a motorcyclist". But can the appeal be analysed? Yes, I am sure it can.

Let's take skiing, for example: In skiing your whole body is involved: Hands, feet, arms legs, torso ... everything. You enjoy the thrill of movement, the wind rushing by, swinging round the curves, battling with the elements. Lady Bracknell would understand and agree with all this but, of course, she would consider skiing patrician, not plebeian!

But the appeal of motorcycling is so similar. Drive a motorcar, no matter how exclusive or expensive and you are sitting in a box. The box may, indeed, have an open top but you are still enclosed in a box. Even in an open car the wind doesn't rush past your face as the windscreen causes a backflow of air that hits the back of your neck; not nearly as pleasant. Most important of all is that you can only control the car with your hands and feet: No use leaning over on the bends.

On a motorcycle, however, as in skiing, you are right out there battling with the elements and as in skiing your whole body is involved; Hands and feet for the controls and your whole body to swing the machine round the bends. In summer the warm air flows past you and in winter, in the right clothing, the battle with the elements begins in earnest but every bit as enjoyable in its own way.

Ride your machine on a summer evening and you experience and enjoy all the scents of the countryside. You ride through the warm air and suddenly hit a patch of colder air, then out into the warmth again. Someone who walks out of his house to travel along the same roads in his car misses all of this.

Everyone remembers the schooldays pleasure of riding their bicycle downhill and swinging it round the bends. With a motorcycle you don't need a downhill gradient as the engine will provide the speed you need. The engine below you provides another of the great pleasures of riding a motorcycle: In good tune it will purr or roar at your command. The foot change gearbox, slicker and quicker than a car, is a joy to use. Getting that gearchange exactly right to suit the conditions and the gradient is a constant and enjoyable challenge.

Come to think of it we might, after all, persuade Lady Bracknell to put her favourite hunter out to grass for a week or two and climb onto a 500cc Triumph Speed Twin. Plebeian? Not with Milady in the saddle!

Motorcycles, too, are not merely a means of transport but a record of twentieth century mechanical and social history. Not only that, but who could deny that they are also examples of twentieth century sculpture? Surely Picasso would have agreed.

The single-geared belt-drive machines ridden by the pioneers in the early days of the century gave them the kind of mobility undreamed of by previous generations. The three-speed chain-cum-belt models of the early 1920's on which the returning servicemen from World War One spent their gratuities gave them the opportunity to exercise their new found mechanical skills. These were put into use on the aeroplanes, cars, motorcycles and lorries during the War years. The late 1920's "saddle tank" models that brought a new look to motorcycles. The early 1930's when design advanced but wages didn't. For so many people in those dreadful depression years there was no wage at all and no job! Then on to the steady advances in design and styling to 1939 together with improving employment prospects.

Post War design continued to race ahead with all leading makers designing their own new vertical twins pioneered by Triumph in the late 1930's up to the race-styled full-fairing four-cylinder Japanese superbikes of today. Compare these with those pioneer single-geared belt drivers from the early years of the century and who could deny that you are looking at social history, mechanical history and twentieth century sculpture.

1937 500cc Triumph Speed Twin. Designed by Edward Turner. With its smooth power delivery, sparkling performance and 90mph top speed it started a design trend that every major motorcycle manufacturer throughout the world had to follow. 25.5bhp at 6,000rpm Price £75.

Pavilion and Paddling Pool

and on the Promenade, lovers of rest may enjoy the sunshine sitting in the hundreds of coloured deck chairs provided for their use, and enjoy the strains of the various military and brass bands playing there.

The Pier—reconstructed—is an ideal rendezvous for those who desire to sit undisturbed, and enjoy their favourite author or novelist with the ripple of the waves beneath them.

RHYL'S AIR WORKS WONDERS

Dolphin Diving from the Pier

Stella Maris is on the other side of the road from the pavilion but not visible in this picture.

Chapter Two
The Beginning

Before World War One my father, John McManus, had started in the cycle business with workshop premises off High Street, Rhyl. At one time he had as many as ninety machines in for repair.

Cycles came into their own in the 1890's. The "Safety" bicycle, in the form that we would recognise as a cycle today, with front and rear wheels the same size and the new pneumatic tyre had arrived at last. About 1900 the free wheel came into use.

So the years 1890 to 1914 saw the great cycling boom which accelerated from 1900. Cycles were used both for work and pleasure: A hitherto undreamed of mobility for everyone had arrived though not all horse owners approved. Writing to "The Times" a retired colonel claimed to have the solution: "I thrust my walking stick into their wheels and bowl them over like pheasants!" But cycles did, at least, have the virtue of silence so the hatred they engendered was as nothing to that inspired by the coming of the motor car.

At the outbreak of War in 1914, however, he and his brothers Tom and Frank immediately volunteered.

He was to serve throughout the War acquiring the rank of Sergeant Major and a leg wound that was to trouble him for the rest of his life! Back from the War, like thousands of others, he had to start again from scratch.

He had met my mother, Norah Utting, during the War at Bedford. He was stationed nearby and my mother worked in the Post Office there. Now married and with a wife to support he started up in business in the same premises, but within a few years they managed to buy a shop in Sussex Street, Rhyl, not far from the High Street and the Promenade. I was born there in August 1923 and my brother Brian in January 1926.

In 1928 they managed to buy 34 West Parade, Rhyl, on the promenade opposite the Pavilion. It was an enormous achievement to have made such a purchase in those difficult years.

My mother came from Shardlow, Derbyshire, and had the benefit of a good secondary education at Long Eaton Grammar School. She was endowed with vision and initiative and was completely unafraid of hard work. She took to business like a duck to water as my wife Edna was to do a quarter of a century later.

34 West Parade was dreadfully run down and neglected when they took over so a marathon of work was required to make it fit to use as a boarding house. The work got done, however, and it was successfully opened for business.

By now my father had gone into partnership with Rhyl entrepreneur Phil Trehearne running the childrens' cycle track on the promenade between Queen Street and High Street. He later moved on to run his own children's cycle track next to the Lifeboat House.

My mother's parents were later to buy the adjoining 35 West Parade but it was soon sold on to my parents when they bought a similar property further along the West Parade, number 75, so another marathon of work was started, combining and refurbishing the two properties.

The problem with this kind of seasonal business is that money comes in during a frantic few months of the year but it goes out for all twelve months! Work, too, is also a 52 week a year job as during the winters all the improvements, redecoration and repairs have to be done.

My mother was determined to see that my brother and I were to have a good education and we were both sent to Rhyl Convent School and later to Epworth College, Rhyl, one of the smaller private schools that competed with the Public Schools in those days.

In my schooldays I spent many holidays, winter and summer, at Glan Clwyd Farm in the Waen about seven miles from Rhyl. Lovely countryside in the incomparable Vale of Clwyd with the River Clwyd flowing past the bottom of the land.

Mrs Davies was a widow who lived there with her son Bobby and daughter Gwen. They were tenants of the Llanerch Estate, now sadly broken up. The rent was £2 an acre, the top price in those days for the best land and that, remember, included the house and buildings. Glan Clwyd Farm was 105 acres. Rents for farms on poorer, sandy soils were as little as ten shillings (50p) an acre. But in those difficult times even good farmers on good land found it hard, or even impossible, to make farming pay.

Bobby Davies, who ran the farm, was a marvellous shot and today he would have made a clay pigeon shot of Olympic standard. In those days, however, every penny was hard earned and there was no question of expending any of those hard earned pennies in busting inedible clay pigeons. Bobby was an excellent shot who enjoyed shooting, but he shot for the pot.

Bobby would send a dog onto one of the few rough bracken covered areas of hillside and the dog would put up a rabbit. Off the rabbit would go, weaving and bouncing over the uneven ground with the dog close behind. Bobby would shoot the rabbit without hesitation every time. I never saw him miss and he never even looked like hitting the dog.

Mrs Davies was a marvellous cook and the rabbits that Bobby shot were roasted with sage and onion stuffing. What a feast they were, served with fresh vegetables; I much preferred them to chicken.

Other than their 1934 Morris van, the only other source of mechanical power was an ancient single cylinder paraffin engine with hot tube ignition. It was only used once a year to grind the corn for winter feed but, amazingly, it always used to start up and run with no trouble.

There was no electric power supply on the farm so Hurricane lanterns were used at night in the buildings and across the yard. In the house the living kitchen had a huge cast iron range with a coal fire. A paraffin lamp with an incandescent mantle gave a surprisingly bright clear light but that was it! Candles provided the light for elsewhere so you went to bed with a lighted candle in its shallow holder and blew it out before you went to sleep.

So all the electric appliances we take for granted today were completely absent and there was no hot water system, just a cold tap in the scullery. A radio, or wireless set as it would have been called then, would have been a possibility, powered by batteries, and would have been of enormous benefit but the Davies' felt they could not afford one. That's how difficult it was to earn a living from farming then.

My own answer to the rabbit problem was to graduate from my airgun to an 1860 .577 calibre military Enfield muzzle loading rifle. I never used it as a rifle, however, with a solid lead bullet but as a shotgun. This was shooting at its most economical: Home-made gunpowder carried in a quarter pound cocoa tin with the bowl of a clay pipe as powder and shot measure.

The clay pipe full of powder would be poured down the barrel and a compressed ball of newspaper rammed down onto it as a wad. The shot charge was poured in next held in by a smaller wad of newspaper. Copper caps to go on the nipple to ignite the charge were too expensive so I used to wedge two paper caps, as used in children's cap guns, into the hammer. These fired the charge perfectly well ... most of the time! On occasion, however, you would get a misfire, which wasn't so bad, or a hangfire.

Hangfires were not so good: The gun would go off as you were taking it from your shoulder! And the shot charge? All sorts of things were used: Second hand ball bearings were quite good, when you could get them. Tin tacks, good but expensive. Gravel, no good at all, don't bother to try it! Home-made pear shaped lead shot? Not very good. How to make it? You don't want to know as it could be dangerous! Finally, of course, lead shot when funds would allow!

So with my trusty muzzle loader was I able to emulate Bobby and pick off those rabbits in front of the dog's nose? Sadly, no; not with the Enfield or anything else. In fact I have never seen such a shot taken by anyone other than Bobby Davies. But did I make a dent in the rabbit population at Glan Clwyd? Again, I'm afraid, the answer has to be "No", but I did knock Hell out of an empty one gallon oil drum!

Farming at Glan Clwyd in the 1930's was a world away from farming today. First of all there were no tractors: Power was supplied by two carthorses, Twm and Jet. There was a small herd of Welsh Mountain sheep and a milking herd of about 25 Shorthorns. The milk was taken daily to Philip Brown, dairyman, of Water Street, Rhyl. Bobby transported it in the 1934 Morris van.

The cows were milked by hand, not milking machine and the regular milk cheque must have been the mainstay of the farm's economy. Most of the land was down to grass though one small field was planted with wheat or barley to help provide winter feed. It was ploughed with a single furrow plough, pulled by Twm and Jet.

Hay, of course, was a most important crop for winter feed. It was all hands to the pumps at hay making time: Twm and Jet would pull the cutter and when the hay was ready they would pull the carts to get the hay back to the farm. Building haystacks by hand was hard going with everyone lending a hand.

I thoroughly enjoyed staying at Glan Clwyd and it gave me a love of farming, forestry and wildlife that has never left me so on leaving school in 1939 a career in farming beckoned.

(Bottom) Cycle Track. My father John McManus at his cycle track on the East Parade Rhyl about 1930. The Lifeboat House is just to the right of the picture but not visible. Note the "Bullnose" pedal car.

(Top) Rhyl pier in the 1930's. Note the long gantry in the foreground enabling the visitors to board the pleasure boats for a "Trip round the bay"

(Bottom) A view of Rhyl from the Voryd. The large light coloured building in the foreground is the Palace Hotel. To the left a block of smaller buildings then the light coloured gable end of my maternal grandparents' house, number 75 West Parade.

Chapter Three
Rhyl in The 1930s

The seaside holiday boom was triggered off by the railways which, for the first time, enabled people to go to the coast on holiday. Former fishing villages were transformed and rows of boarding houses were quickly built on the sea fronts. The 1860's and 70's were boom years and most seaside towns were built in the same style. Rhyl was a typical example.

Overseas holidays were only for the very wealthy so the seaside towns provided holidays for all. This continued up to the first World War and into the nineteen twenties and thirties, too. The dreadful slump of the early thirties brought the country to its knees and Rhyl, of course, did not escape. Money was scarce for holidays but Rhyl did manage to limp along and although times were undoubtedly hard they were nothing like as bad as in the industrial areas. Even so, people at the bottom of the heap, even in Rhyl, didn't get enough to eat. Hard times today bear no comparison to hard times then.

For those with money, Rhyl was a marvellous place to be but the problem was that hardly anyone had much of it! To stay at Stella Maris in the thirties cost between two and a half and three and a half guineas a week. That doesn't sound much but that sum took a lot of finding for the majority of people.

Despite hard times, Rhyl did all it could to pull in the punters: For good measure there was the location with the Vale of Clwyd at its back and the wide stretch of sandy beach in front. But, of course, holidaymakers have to be entertained and there was no shortage.

The Rhyl Pavilion was the most important place of entertainment with all kinds of shows and, in addition, a resident band during the summer. Even in the winter time the Pavilion kept busy with shows, trade exhibitions, events of all kinds and Armitage Owen's Manchester Repertory Company. There were two concert parties: Will Parkin's "Coliseum", an open air show of surprising quality and Billy Manders' Quaintesques in the "Amphitheatre" at the foot of the pier. They put on some cracking shows. Billie Manders was a female impersonator from, I believe, the Birmingham area originally. The shows were hugely enjoyable with sketches, music, the whole fun of a seaside pierrot show. Elwyn Edwards' tenor voice was always a feature and there was, in the middle of the show, an interlude when all the performers transformed themselves into the resident band. The comedian, Jimmy Wright, took over the drums with enthusiasm and they turned out great musical entertainment.

It was also the age of the cinema and Rhyl was well provided: The "Royal" at the top of High Street was an older building converted into a cinema and the "Queens" on the promenade was remarkably stylish.

In the early thirties a new cinema was built, the "Plaza" halfway down the High Street: A magnificent new building and a prime example of a modern picture palace with magnificent decor and carpets. I believe that the first film shown was "Fire over England" with Flora Robson as Queen Elizabeth: Regarded, at the time, as a monumental epic, but we schoolboys found it boring!

Another new cinema in the mid thirties was the "Regal" further down the High Street and, of course, the new "Odeon" at the bottom which aspired to the highest standards.

For we schoolboys the entertainment in the town was an important part of our lives. We visited the many shows and plays at the Pavilion and, of course, a weekly visit to the cinema was not to be missed. There were many films which were later to be regarded as classics which still continue to come back on T.V. to this day. Many, though by no means all, have stood the test of time remarkably well.

We youngsters loved humour and chortled uncontrollably at the antics of the comedians of the day such as Will Hay with his companions Graham Moffatt, the fat young one and Moore

Marriott, the half witted old one. George Formby, too, was a great favourite: The gormless Lancashire lad who, against all the odds, always got the girl in the end!

The decade started with Greta Garbo in her first talking role "Anna Christie" and her first husky voiced line "Gimme a visky with ginger ale on the side...and don't be stingy, baby."

Another newcomer, Marlene Deitrich, smouldered as the cabaret singer in "The Blue Angel". The great anti-war film "All Quiet on the Western Front" by Erich Maria Remarque is still moving today. Noel Coward's "Cavalcade", depicting English life since the turn of the century caught the mood of the times and Charlie Chaplin's "City Lights" still fought a rearguard action against the new "talkies" by making it a silent film.

Shirley Temple, aged four, started her amazing career and Fred Astaire made his debut. It is reputed that after his screen test he was described thus: "Can't act, can't sing, can dance a little". His teaming with Ginger Rogers in "The Gay Divorcee" created a dazzling dance partnership that has never been surpassed. "Cole Porter's "Night and Day" was the unforgettable song from the film. This was followed by Jerome Kern's "Roberta" with "Smoke Gets in your Eyes" and the smash hit "Top Hat". Irving Berlin wrote the title number and the immortal "Cheek to Cheek".

In the mid thirties Rochdale's Gracie Fields, "Our Gracie", was paid an unprecedented £150,000 for three films. She said "I don't really like it. There's too much responsibility. Give me a cottage and ten shillings!"

The great movie mogul, Alexander Korda, produced "The "Private Life of Henry VIII" starring Charles Laughton followed by "Rembrandt".

Late in the decade Walt Disney surprised the world with his first full length cartoon film, "Snow White and the Seven Dwarfs". Up to that time it was generally thought that cartoon films would never progress beyond short interludes between main features, but Disney took a huge gamble with two million drawings and three years work. His faith was rewarded with the film's resounding success. He had introduced "Mickey Mouse" to the screen in 1928.

When Neville Chamberlain returned from his meeting with Hitler in late 1938 he carried the peace agreement made between

England and Germany. Cheering crowds gathered outside Downing Street to hear him say "I believe it is peace in our time". As someone said however "Peace in our time, but his or mine? For I am only twenty three and he is sixty nine!".

Chamberlain has often been criticised, derided even, for that Munich agreement, but I have never subscribed to this view. It did give the country another year to prepare for war and this opportunity was definitely grasped. Chamberlain himself knew perfectly well that the agreement was not written on tablets of stone and he had many reservations, though it would not have been politic to make them public at that time. In any event the public desperately wanted peace and this was the only possible decision which did give the country hope. Yes, I know that Ralph Waldo Emerson said that "Hope is the folded tram ticket placed under the wobbly table leg of life" and in 1938 that table leg was unusually wobbly, but its purpose was served.

Rhyl was a marvellous place for a child to grow up in the nineteen twenties and thirties. Even without a lot of money to spend, there were still many advantages. Brian and I, living on the promenade opposite the Pavilion, were especially fortunate.

Donkeys jingling along the sands with their excited crowd of cheering children. Pleasure boats coming up to the beach on the incoming tide to take the holidaymakers a trip out into Liverpool Bay.

Amusement arcades along the promenade with their seductive slot machines soliciting pennies from the holidaymakers...and the local children! Cafes with their advertising blackboards outside pulling in the punters for a three course meal at one shilling and sixpence (seven and a half pence). Motor coaches offering trips to all locations in North Wales. Most expensive a whole day return trip to Snowdon with lunch provided at seven shillings and sixpence (thirty seven and a half pence).

At the lifeboat house the slogan then, as now, was "Supported entirely by voluntary contributions". The lifeboat, the "Caroline Richardson" was man-powered. No engine: It had to be rowed by two rows of oarsmen reminiscent of "Ben Hur". It was built in the 1890's and still in use in 1939 and was, I believe, the longest serving lifeboat in the Country. No cover of any kind to give protection from the elements and the slatted floor meant the crew were open to the sea under their feet. Peculiar twin pod construction not unlike a monster version of today's rubber boats.

A far cry from today's "Mersey" class self righting boats powered by twin turbocharged diesels but the "Caroline Richardson, self righting? Not a chance!

A tourist attraction on a sunny summer's day to tempt the visitors to put pennies into the collection boxes but what must it have been like for the crew to launch it on a pitch black winter's night, facing heavy seas and stinging sleet driven by a Northerly gale? Think about it! The lifeboat men then, as now, all part-time volunteers.

On a summer day the whole length of the promenade would be lined with cars, motorcycles and motorcycles and sidecars because notwithstanding the competition of a new or secondhand Austin Seven the motorcycle combination was still very much in the picture. The types of sidecar covered a tremendous number of styles with "Launch" sidecars being very popular, rather like a small boat with imitation decking and foghorn type ventilators.

"Oh I do like to be beside the sea side
I do like to be beside the sea.
I do like to stroll along the prom, prom, prom
While the Brass Band plays tiddley om, pom, pom."

Reginald Dixon's signature tune on the organ from the Tower Ballroom Blackpool...and how we enjoyed those broadcasts.

Now you could not have a seaside town without a brass band, certainly not in pre-War days and Rhyl went one better with Rhyl Silver Band.

I have always considered brass bands to be the musical equivalent of an elephant dancing but I will concede that they are an essential sound at the seaside. Rhyl had a bandstand on the promenade and you really could stroll along the prom, prom, prom while the brass (silver) band played.....

Just across the road to the left of the Pavilion was the Rhyl paddling pool so all we had to do to get there was to walk across the road. As small children we spent many happy hours there. Model yachts were sailed enthusiastically and they sailed very well indeed.

Just beyond the paddling pool was the sea wall and the beach, so off we would go with buckets and spades to build sand castles or with jam jar and nets to catch shrimps or the tiny fish left in the sandy pools by the receding tide. So there was an enormous world of childhood enjoyment right on our doorstep.

Children digging on the sands, sunlight sparkling on the summer sea, the attraction of the Marine Lake pleasure beach with it's roller coaster, miniature steam train and every kind of ride and side-show. Everyone in holiday mood and that mood was infectious.

So was the winter an anticlimax? Not at all: in winter you had the place to yourself so winter had a charm of its own.

I was born on August 18th. 1923 and went to the local convent school, moving to Epworth College, Rhyl in 1934, leaving in 1939. Epworth gave you a worth while start because not only did it have an excellent, dedicated teaching staff but you were in a company of winners who were keen to learn and were going to get on in life. I am sure that most boys went on to do well.

I was a day boy but most were boarders. My great friends were John Kimberley Tully (Twirley) and John Phillips (Fatty). J.K.T. was from a single parent family and lived with his mother; they were from a theatrical background. J.K.T. was to go on to become a writer and journalist. John Phillips' father was a widower and they lived in a very pleasant house in the road opposite to the Convent playing field. His father was a bank manager and John, too, was to go into the Midland Bank.

My mother ran the boarding house at 34/35 West Parade and my father ran the children's cycle track near the lifeboat house. Sixpence (2 1/pence) for half an hour was the rate! In the winter he would refurbish the bikes ready for the next season.

My father never owned a car or motorcycle as it was only the privileged few who could aspire to a car in those days. Not many people owned a motorcycle, either, and there was no motorcycle dealer in Rhyl.

The local sports shop, Nelson Brothers in Queen Street had dealt in motorcycles in the past but when I was a boy all they had were Scott Cyc-Autos, price nineteen guineas: An impossible figure for us in those days. We had cycles, of course, and thoroughly enjoyed riding them but we used to look admiringly at those autocycles and think how marvellous it would be to own one: To be able to ride without pedalling... bliss! Amazingly, however, I

16

didn't know anyone who owned a motorcycle so there was no-one to talk to about them.

Although money was never plentiful for almost everyone in those years, we were more fortunate than most. We were never in any way deprived nor did we ever go short of anything. Birthdays and Christmases were always magical with no shortage of presents.

As we got older we played all the childhood games as they came into season: Marbles would be all the rage to be followed by whips and tops. Then there would be conker fights followed by the yo-yo craze that swept the country. We all had them and some of the youngsters became really expert with them.

Older still we were able to build model aeroplanes and, once again, some boys were really good at it. No miniature engines in those days, the models were rubber powered. I remember the "Wakefield" models with square section fuselages. They made no attempt to copy a real aeroplane but with their slowly rotating rubber powered propellers they could fly surprising distances. Scale models, too, could often fly well with the high wing monoplanes the easiest to build and fly.

When we discovered reading a new world stretched before us. The "Comics" of the day, price twopence, were enormously popular: The "Wizard", "Modern Boy", "Hotspur", "Rover", "Bullseye" and many others. Biggles, flying his Sopwith Camel in the pages of the "Modern Boy" was one of our favourite heroes.

The Biggles stories were also published as books and were written by Captain W.E. Johns who had himself flown Sopwith Camels on the Western Front in World War One. A fellow pilot in his squadron was a Derby man named Wigglesworth who was, of course, inevitably called "Wiggles". When W.E. Johns wanted a hero for his fictional war stories he was prompted by the thought of "Wiggles" so he named his hero "Bigglesworth", shortened to "Biggles".

In the "Magnet" we read about the "Famous five" in Greyfriars "Remove": Bob Cherry, Harry Wharton, Hurree Jamset Ram Singh and others with the most famous character of all, Billy Bunter.

Onto hardbacks our great favourites were the "William" books written by Richmal Crompton. William was the anarchic schoolboy rebel with his inseparable friends, "The Outlaws", together with his dog "Jumble". The lisping Violet Elizabeth Bott with her propensity to "schream and schream and schream" provided the schoolgirl, but definitely not romantic, interest.

We also thoroughly enjoyed the romantic historical romances by Jeffrey Farnol, usually set in the period of the French Revolution and then graduated to the hard stuff by Baroness Orczy, such as "The Scarlet Pimpernel"

"Beau Geste" by P.C. Wren was one of our great favourites, a stirring story of the French Foreign Legion which was destined to be filmed many times.

We also attempted to tackle some of the classics but found them quite unreadable: Cervantes' Don Quixote was a perfect example. I then attempted to read "The Hunchback Notre Dame" by Victor Hugo but having waded through the first fifty pages, devoted entirely to describing the crowd scene outside Notre Dame, I gave it best and gave up! "Monopoly" came over from the United States in the mid thirties and we became fanatical, and sometimes furious, players. A marvellous game but, all too often, the cause of excited arguments! Meccano and Hornby trains were perennial favourites. I had a tank engine in L.N.E.R. green with a good length of track and trackside accessories to provide many hours of pleasure. Model soldiers, too, were great favourites and we amassed a substantial collection.

Another craze that hit us was cinematography. We had 16mm silent projectors with odd lengths of film. We gave impromptu film shows for all our friends with a sheet for a screen.

(Top) 1939 "Ladies Model" Scott Cyc-Auto. Price £19.19s. We looked longingly at them through Nelsons shop window and dreamed of gliding along without having to pedal.
(Bottom) Early 1930's Two seater Austin Seven as owned by our Science Master, E.A. Beet.

(Top) One of the miniature **steam** trains that took holidaymakers
round the Marine Lake.
(Bottom) Beach fashions of the 1930's at Rhyl. Do you think they
will ever come back?

Chapter Four
Family Affairs

My father's family had been in Rhyl for generations so we had the benefit of an extended family. This was an advantage we simply took for granted, never realising, at the time, how fortunate we were. We had uncles, aunts and cousins and were very close to them all.

Most men of my father's age had served in the Great War, 1914 to 1918. Those that were fortunate enough to come back had to start their lives again from scratch but many were to suffer from the effects of the War for the rest of their lives.

My father received a few shillings a week pension for his leg injury. His brother, Tom, was in exactly the same boat as he, too, had a leg injury. Youngest brother Frank was, perhaps, the worst injured of all but his injury was psychological, not physical.

In a way the War was good to him in that he was never badly injured and he was a brilliantly successful soldier, rising to the rank of captain. When fighting in the Middle East he met the legendary Lawrence of Arabia and his most vivid memory of Lawrence was his favourite expression "Don't fuss, don't fuss" when all Hell was let loose.

But like so many others who had progressed successfully in the Army, the return to civilian life was a disaster and his full potential was never to be realised again. He had adapted to officer status "As to the manner born". Unfortunately, however, unlike many of his fellow officers, there was no manor with its accompanying estate and income waiting for him after the War. He was still quite obviously a member of the officer class who could speak knowledgeably, and with a cut glass accent, about building up a shoot or investing in the Stock Market, but without the wherewithal to put any of it into practical effect. A permanently damaged leg would have been a far kinder fate.

We saw a lot of our uncle Frank and we admired his heavy Webley service revolver which he kept at home, though it was never fired. A small compensation for him was his role in the local Territorial Army where he retained officer rank and took an active part, always going to summer camp with them but, of course, it was a pale shadow of the real thing.

Frank never married but lived with his unmarried sister, Agnes, in their tiny house on Vale Road, Rhyl. My father's other brother, Tom, worked with him and he had three children, a boy and two girls. My brother Brian was always very close to Uncle Tom and he spent many miles riding on the crossbar of Tom's bike, often singing happily away.

Tom and his wife lived in one of those huge Victorian houses at Pensarn, just along the coast from Rhyl. Tom travelled to and fro on his cycle. Pensarn was a place that had not only missed the bus but had, unfortunately, not missed the train. In the Victorian seaside holiday boom when the rows of identical three storey terraced boarding houses were being erected on sea fronts all over the British Isles, Pensarn did the same. The trouble was that they had to be erected behind the railway line, not in front of it as it was too close to the shore. Pensarn started with a dreadful handicap that it was never able to overcome. It has never developed as a successful seaside resort. Behind Pensarn was Abergele but this was too far from the beach for holidaymakers.

My father had three sisters: Agnes who was unmarried and Mary and Catherine who were both married. To us they were Auntie Sullivan and Auntie Rainbow. Their husbands, however, were simply "Uncle" to us and addressed by their wives not as "Patrick" and "Herbert" but as "Sullivan" and "Rainbow" respectively. Both were kindly men who had, like all their contemporaries, served in the War. Before going to France Uncle Sullivan had achieved distinction as the best shot in the regiment, an achievement of which he was justly proud.

Auntie Rainbow had a fierce demeanour and we were always in awe of her. Auntie Sullivan was altogether different: A rotund, cheery person always delighted to see us. The Sullivans had an only daughter, older than us, named Mary. Mary was always stage-struck and loved to take part in every kind of amateur dramatics and produced impromptu plays with her school friends.

The Rainbows had a son and a daughter, Bert and Eileen who, once again, were older than us. Bert was a brilliant footballer and played outside left for the Welsh schoolboy team on a number of occasions. Bert was a very pleasant youngster and very good to we smaller cousins, as was his sister Eileen.

The most important part of those days was, of course, school. Brian and I started at the Convent, Rhyl. We found the nuns very strict but this might have been necessary with spirited youngsters. So did we learn anything? I'm sure we did: Happiest memory is Brian's realisation that vous avez rhymed with boozer bay!

Sister Mary Edmund was the nun who taught us and she firmly believed that to spare the rod was to spoil the child! Bruce Slinn, son of a local dentist, used to make sure that Sister Mary Edmund was well within earshot but not looking our way and then give me a vicious punch in the small of the back.

Obviously I would howl with anguish and punch him back, whereupon Sister Mary Edmund would cane me for "fighting". She could wield that cane to devastating effect and it was extremely painful.

Naturally I complained about the injustice: Bruce had hit me first and provoked retaliation so why was he not caned, too? Her answer was always the same: Bruce's blows were only "Love taps" so did not merit punishment. But how did she know? Bruce was always careful to ensure that she wasn't looking when he launched that punch! An early lesson for me that "There ain't no justice".

The important move was to Epworth College on the outskirts of Rhyl on the Rhuddlan Road. Epworth had been started by Joseph Beatty who was getting old when we commenced school. He was a great Shakespearean scholar and in our later days he would sometimes take us for lessons on Shakespeare's plays. George Brooks reminds me that I had the temerity to argue with him over the interpretation of some passages, but I must say I can't remember it. In fact I remember him as being most helpful in helping us to understand and enjoy Shakespeare's works.

Epworth was run by Joseph Beatty's son, Philip H. Beatty. Boys were taken through the school system to School Certificate and Matriculation standard.

You were not dragged down by a percentage who not only had no intention of learning but were determined to hinder others. With no such distractions we could get on with the job. The masters were all excellent and dedicated to doing their utmost to enable us to achieve our best potential.

The headmaster, Philip Beatty, taught English and inspired in us all a love of literature. Smith-Stafford, an extrovert with an Oxford degree, taught geography. A man with an outstanding personality and an inspired teacher. He was later to be killed at Dunkirk. He attempted to explain to us an amazing theory: The British Empire, far from being an enormous benefit to the country was, in reality, a drag on it. We did not believe a word of it; surely we "owned" all those vast areas coloured pink on the map of the world?

E.A. Beet taught science, a subject that interested us all. He had been educated at Epworth before going on to University.

Epworth had a remarkably good science laboratory where we toiled with our spring balances and Bunsen burners. He had a tiny open two seater Austin or Morris of about 1930 vintage which only came out on high days and holidays. Astronomy was his great interest and he had written a book on the subject when he was twenty nine and was to go on to write another seven. He became the President of the British Astronomical Society and in retirement he was the Astronomical Correspondent for "The Times".

Once when he was lecturing to our class I had a Number Three bore garden gun cartridge cap under the desk. They are large rimfire cartridges so I was pricking off the paper backing to expose the percussion powder beneath. Suddenly it exploded with a tremendous bang and shot across the classroom giving us all, including Mr. Beet, a tremendous shock!

Those days at Epworth were most enjoyable and we were all very fortunate indeed to have been educated there.

A Joint Game of Bowls

from Mr. P. C. Crompton, Water Street, Rhyl. The reservoirs at Llanefydd are well stocked with trout, and permission to fish therein can be obtained from the Water Dept., Clwyd Street, Rhyl.

HORSEBACK RIDING.

This type of sport is becoming more and more attractive, owing to the fine stretch of sands at Rhyl.
Details of Riding Schools may be had on application to the Publicity Office, Town Hall, Rhyl.

_____

" RHYL'S AIR WILL DO YOU
A WORLD OF GOOD."

Morning Gallop

After a "Spot" of Fishing

Bowls on the East Parade. The lady disembarking from the "Prince of Wales" onto one of the mobile gantries looks none too steady!

(Top) 504K. Famous Two Seater Training Aircraft of the 1914/18 War. It was made in various forms and carried out the first planned bombing raid in the history of warfare when three of them bombed the airship sheds at Friedrickshafen on November 21st. 1914. Early models were fitted with the Gnome 80hp rotary engine. These ex RAF planes gave visitors trips from Kinmel bay beach to Rhyl pier and back at five shillings per flight.
(Bottom) The 1917 D.H. 9 bomber, a development of the D.H. 4. Initially unsuccessful due to engine problems but eventually successful with Siddeley Puma engines of 270hp. It continued in service in some air forces up to the 1930's. I had my first flight in an Ex RAF machine, price one shilling.

Chapter Five
Entertainment at Rhyl

An unusual trip offered to visitors were flights from Kinmel Bay over Rhyl beach to the pier and back. They were in World War One Avro 504K aircraft and the price was five shillings per trip. So throughout the summer days these planes would roar over the holidaymakers on Rhyl beach before making a banking turn over the pier for the return journey.

But in the 1930's a regular feature of the summer season was the arrival of the flying circuses which were always held on the wide, flat fields from Kinmel Bay to the Borth cross-roads. Alan Cobham's was probably the most famous of all but there were many others.

When the flying circuses arrived they were occasions not to be missed: All kinds of flying displays were on show: mock combats, balloon busting (Toy balloons, not the observer balloons famous from World War One), displays of aerial acrobatics, parachute jumping and much more. All done in ancient aeroplanes, mostly of World War One vintage.

At one of these events it was announced that passengers would be given a flight for the bargain price of one shilling instead of the normal two shillings. Never having raised the five shillings for a flight from Kinmel Bay, now was my chance. The plane was a World War One D.H. 9 bomber. It bumped along the grass surface then suddenly the bumping stopped and we were airborne: A wonderful moment in a flight that more than fulfilled all my expectations.

During the summer time you would hear the sound of distant trumpets and the rumble of drums: It was a parade marching along the promenade. Great excitement as we all crowded to watch. There seemed to be an endless number of parades given by all sorts of outfits that would be in summer camp nearby, usually on the Rhyl to Abergele road. The Territorials, the Church Lads Brigade and, as far as I know, The Flat Earth Society and many others would hold these parades entertaining both residents and visitors alike.

On the other end of the scale there was the Salvation Army whose small groups would gather outside the pubs on a Saturday night to sing, accompanied by the mournful notes of their cornet player. You had to give them full marks for dedication because the question had to be asked whether or not these outdoor musical events ever actually "converted" anyone? A requirement for the girls, we decided, was that they had to be very plain indeed! Or was it that the deliberately designed ultra frumpish uniform would have made Marlene Deitrich look plain? But regardless of any obstacles, the Church Army soldiered on.

But when it came to religion, Rhyl suffered from an "Embarras des richesses". The place was crammed full of churches, chapels and places of worship of every possible description. If there was a society for The Propagation Of The Gospel By One-Legged Vegetarian Ex-Licensee Welsh Victuallers, then they would have had a chapel in Rhyl and in that chapel would be a bell to add its dolorous clanging to the solemn Sabbath!

Although the majority of business people in Rhyl were English the town was, after all, in Wales, so despite being a seaside town with its raison d'être to cater for and entertain visitors, when Sundays arrived the Welsh chapel ethic was applied. No pubs, for example, were allowed to open on a Sunday.

The biggest church in the town was the Church of England's St. Thomas' and on Sundays all churches and chapels vied with each other in their tolling of innumerable bells. Their discordant, depressing jangle endowed us with a hatred of church bells that could never be eradicated in a lifetime. There are, I understand, some people who actually like church bells and can even be persuaded to ring the accursed things, but they would have been permanently cured if they had spent a Sunday or two in Rhyl in the nineteen thirties! Apart from uncles, aunts and cousins we had second cousins, more distant relatives and, no doubt, third cousins quadrupally removed! They all added to our circle of friends plus, of course, the many families with whom my father's family had been friends from way back when. So to be a member of a community with so many friends and relatives was a great bonus.

As we lived in a holiday town my mother's relatives from Derbyshire would often visit and were always made welcome by my mother's generous hospitality so we were kept well in touch with them, too.

A friend of mine was Vernon Trehearne. He was a few years older than me and his father, Philip was one of Rhyl's most successful entrepreneurs. Even in those days he had started to put together the family's huge block of property and business interests on Rhyl promenade. Vernon, even as a schoolboy, was a budding entrepreneur and was to go on to expand these interests.

On one occasion, when I was about ten, Vernon decided that we youngsters would put on a big display of model soldiers on the sands. Sand forts would be constructed and the soldiers would be arranged in an eye catching display. A hat would be strategically placed and all contributions would be gratefully received.

We all brought our soldiers along and before we started Vernon asked us all individually how much we wanted for our contribution at the end of the day's display. I said sixpence and, with a nod of his head, Vernon agreed. Others requested a more ambitious sum! We all, however, knew what we were going to earn.

Vernon, of course, was the financier: If the total take was less than the amount Vernon had agreed to pay out, then he would have to make up the difference out of his own pocket. If more, then Vernon would be entitled to the surplus. We made an excellent, eye-catching display and the visitors were both appreciative and generous: Vernon's vision was vindicated!

In the summer time Rhyl business families were far too busy to give children's' parties but in the winter it was party time, and what marvellous fun they were. Vernon's parties were second to none and I still look back on them with great appreciation. They were boys' parties with silly girls not being even thought of. Funny how, in a few years time, we were not to think of girls as silly after all!

But those parties were absolutely tremendous fun with lots to eat and drink, party games galore and, of course, fights! Joyous, happy, light-hearted fights when there would be a pile of boys rolling all over the floor, a flailing mass of arms and legs. No-one ever got hurt in these good-humoured fights but how we enjoyed them, ending up thoroughly happy, panting, dishevelled and with ties askew.

A childhood in Rhyl left me, as previously explained, with an eternal dislike of church bells and there was another phobia: Shellfish. Shellfish were never served at Stella Maris yet shrimps, shellfish and oysters were very much part of the scene in a seaside town. Vendors would walk along the beach offering oysters for sale and we watched in wonder as they were split open and the contents poured down the victim's, sorry, gourmet's throat. If it had happened to me the contents would undoubtedly have come up again faster than they had gone down in the first place.

Brian and I used to dig for cockles in the sandy gullies off the East Parade when the tide was out for which we earned coppers rather than shillings. Were we paid twopence a pound or twopence a ton? Can't remember, but it was not very lucrative. Even so, those extra coppers were most welcome. It's hard to believe but Brian could actually cook and eat the things, though he cannot remember it now, but for me the very thought of their sewage sustained contents was enough to induce a fit of nausea!

As far as I am concerned, then, cockles, mussels, whelks, oysters, winkles, shrimps, jellied eels and all others of that ilk are off the menu.....and don't mention church bells!

But at the other end of the scale there were, indeed, some very good things to eat at Rhyl. Many grocers in Rhyl in those days baked their own bread and much of it was really delicious.

Ice cream, too, was made by many of the cafes and we considered that made by the Sidoli's in Wellington Road to be the best of all, and they are still going today, followed by the Viola on the opposite side of the road who came a very close second. But Sidoli's coffee was unsurpassed. Try it when you are next in Rhyl.

"Never ask for whom the bell tolls; it tolls for thee"

As long as we agree, that's thee, not me!

(Top) West Parade Rhyl about 1930. My maternal grandparents' house is the first house on the right hand side at the corner of Butterton Road. Armitage Owen had the first floor flat there, overlooking the promenade, while he was at Rhyl.
(Bottom) During the winters of the late 1930's and early 1940's, W. Armitage Owen and his Manchester Repertory Company presented plays at the Rhyl Pavilion. The members of his company shown here included Moira Manners, Amanda Whitehead, Elizabeth Kirby, Horace Wentworth, Dorothy Edwards, Mary Gauntlett, Norman Prince, Gerald Pemberton, Joseph Holroyd and Edna Morris. Edna Morris appeared in Albert Finney's "Saturday Night and Sunday Morning", 1960, as did a motorcycle combination supplied by us!

The Swimming Pool

RHYL'S greatest amenity, and one of the finest open-air Swimming Pools in England and Wales.

It is 110 yards long and 30 yards wide, and contains three-quarters-of-a million gallons of water, which is filtered continually at the rate of 95,000 gallons per hour.

Without doubt, it is the most popular feature of all the Council's enterprises. Situated on the East Promenade, the Swimming Pool has accommodation for 400 bathers and 5,000 spectators—no expense has been spared for the comfort and safety of its patrons. The bath is shallow at both ends, and is equipped with every modern aquatic apparatus—rafts, chutes and diving boards. Experienced Life-Guards, under the control of an efficient Superintendent, patrol the bath sides. Cleanliness is a noted feature. Foothaths are provided in the cubicles, and all towels are laundered and sterilized in the Bath's up-to-date laundry. Floodlight bathing is a great attraction, and throughout the season Illuminated Galas are a weekly feature. At these may be seen some of England's greatest swimmers and divers, while the displays of fire-works are a sight to be remembered. Occasionally beautiful Manne-quins, wearing the latest in beach and bathing attire, parade its banks, to the appreciation of the specta-tors. A Cafe of Continental design supplies the needs of both bather and specta-tor, while orchestral and dance music entertains you.

BE IN THE SWIM.

*Fireworks,
Rhyl Swimming Pool*

The Swimming Pool

Rhyl was very proud of its open air baths, built in the early 1930's

Chapter Six
1939 and All That

1939 was a vintage year: Lawrence Olivier and Merle Oberon starred in William Wyler's "Wuthering Heights" and seventeen year old Judy Garland appeared in the immortal "Wizard of Oz". Leslie Howard and Wendy Hiller appeared in George Bernard Shaw's "Pygmalion" which gained an Academy Award. "Ridiculous" said G.B.S. "I have already received credit for the play!"

Robert Donat was the heart-warming master in "Goodbye Mr Chips", in which the scenes showing the boys returning to school as the years rolled by were filmed outside the ancient arch at the entrance to Repton School, Derbyshire and for good measure, Charles Laughton starred as the never to be forgotten hunchback in Victor Hugo's "The Hunchback of Notre Dame".

But 1939 produced one of the greatest blockbusters of all time, "Gone With The Wind", an American Civil War epic starring Clark Gable and Vivien Leigh.

All the films mentioned above are, of course, only a brief synopsis of the huge range of films produced: Westerns, historical romances and adventures, foreign intrigue, flying, detective films from Sherlock Holmes to tough Hollywood Private Eyes and many others. Surely Basil Rathbone and Nigel Bruce are the definitive Holmes and Watson. Horror, too, with "Dracula" and the ever sinister Boris Karloff as the never to be forgotten Frankenstein's monster.

But of all the heroic swashbucklers, none swashed a buckle as dashingly as Errol Flynn with his ideal screen partner, Olivia de Haviland. In everything from westerns to historical adventure, he was the greatest. His "Robin Hood" with Olivia de Haviland in 1939 has never been surpassed: Kevin Costner, eat your heart out!

The radio, or wireless as we called it in the 1930's, was a very important part of our life. Plays, current affairs, variety, documentaries and, not least, music. No television in those days so the wireless was of great importance in any home.

Arthur Askey and Richard Murdoch had a situation comedy in which they occupied a fictional flat on the roof of Broadcasting House, London and we thoroughly enjoyed those programmes.

On Saturday evenings there was always a variety programme: comedians, music, all sorts of speciality acts that relied on sound, not vision.

"In Town Tonight" was another very popular Saturday night programme when celebrities and other interesting personalities who were in London i.e. "in town tonight" were interviewed.

We youngsters, of course, thoroughly enjoyed the music of the period and the radio provided it. It was the Big Band era and we heard them all on radio and saw many of them at Rhyl Pavilion: Roy Fox, Geraldo, Henry Hall, Carol Gibbons, Jack Hylton, Jack Payne and Joe Loss to name but a few. Jack Payne and, later, Henry Hall conducted the BBC Dance Orchestra.

As we youngsters were keen radio fans much time and energy was expended in building our own radios. We would have a plywood baseboard and a plywood front mounted vertically against it. The works i.e. valves, resistors, coils etc. would be mounted on these wooden surfaces. Our simple radios would usually be two valve sets and powered by batteries: An HT dry battery and a low voltage acid battery. They had to have an outside aerial and earth and rigging up an aerial could be a problem.

But did they work? Yes, they did, usually with a primitive "cone" loudspeaker placed away from the set. Crystal sets, too, were tackled where a piece of energised crystal (don't ask me what it was), provided the power. Although they did, indeed, work you had to have earphones and the sound was, as you would expect, very faint.

I left Epworth in the summer of 1939 with a School Certificate. An ideal time, then, at age sixteen, to metaphorically dip my toe in the water and confirm whether or not farming as a career would be a good idea. The problem was that instead of dipping my toe in the water I tripped up, went in headfirst at the deep end, banging my head on the bottom for good measure!

I elected to go onto a farm on the Abergele to Bodelwyddan road and as I was there to gain experience I worked alongside the men for the normal working day which was 6 A.M. to 6 P.M. This meant getting up at about 5.30 A.M. so for someone having just left school this was a tremendous shock to the system! As I was there for the experience it was obviously without pay though board and lodgings were provided.

When Noel Coward was asked to comment on an unusual, bizarre or outlandish person or happening he would invariably reply "Remarkable!" A marvellous answer of consummate diplomacy as it gave the questioner the opportunity to interpret it in exactly the way that suited him: Remarkably good or remarkably bad? The answer diplomatically covered both extremes.

The farmer I have no hesitation in describing as "Remarkable".

There were two farm workers employed there: Evan, pronounced Eee-van and a younger man who lived in. He was very Welsh, as was Evan and the farmer and his name was Iorwerth. How do you pronounce Iorwerth? Use your imagination and don't hesitate to drum roll those r's ! All three were Welsh speakers.

Both Evan and Iorwerth were very kind to me. Evan was married and lived in a tied cottage. His wage was £2.10s (Two pounds fifty pence) per week and his rent free cottage. Iorwerth was unmarried and his wage was £1.5s (One pound twenty five pence) per week and his keep. Incredible how low wages were then, even taking inflation into account. Tax for Iorwerth's 350cc motorcycle was £3.15s per year so it took three week's work, working his normal six day week at twelve hours a day (216 hours) to pay for it. Don't tell today's Chancellor of the Exchequer!

I found the heavy work and those dreadfully long hours very hard going indeed but one sunny morning the farmer asked me if I would like to go with him to see some cattle; obviously I jumped at the chance.

Off we went in his car to Abergele then the long uphill pull towards Llanfair Talhaiarn. (Now try pronouncing that!) Next a downhill stretch to the bottom of the valley followed by a right turn.

After travelling some distance along that stretch of road he turned uphill onto a farm track.

He disappeared into the farmhouse and left me to it: I didn't see any cattle!

After lengthy negotiations I finally saw him again, this time accompanied by the farmer driving six or eight bullocks. Taking a stick out of the back of the car he handed it to me and told me to drive the beasts home.

Now this was the very first time that I had any idea that I would be landed with such a task and it was a "remarkable" decision: For a start it was really a two man job, one in front and one behind but I had to do it on my own. When a car came I had to get the beasts out of the way and at every drive or side turning the animals turned into it so I had to get them back. The distance was twelve miles or more but the distance I actually walked, or ran, was nearer double that.

To make things even worse I had to drive them through the top of Abergele. I had nothing to eat or, more importantly, drink since breakfast, so by the time I got back to the farm in late afternoon I was absolutely exhausted. It was also "remarkable" that boy and beasts all arrived intact and uninjured!

That was the beginning of the end of my stay at the Abergele farm. In any case, the punishing work was beginning to take its toll and my neck had erupted into a mass of boils. The idea of a career in farming no longer had quite the same appeal, especially under those conditions.

Stella Maris, 34/35 West Parade, opposite the pavilion. Third and fourth houses to the left of Edward Henry Street.

H.J. 117709

MOTOR FUEL RATION BOOK
FOR THE MONTHS OF MAY, JUNE AND JULY, 1941

M/C OVER 250 c.c.

Motor Cycle
(including Tricycle)

Registered Number of Vehicle

RA 1489

Date and Office of Issue

The coupons in this book authorise the furnishing and acquisition of the number of units of motor fuel specified on the coupons.

The issue of a Ration Book does not guarantee to the holder any minimum quantity of motor fuel and the coupons contained in this book may be cancelled at any time without notice.

Any person furnishing or acquiring motor fuel otherwise than in accordance with the provisions of the Order for the time being in force under which these coupons are issued or contrary to the conditions appearing thereon will be liable to prosecution.

51-7457. S.P. & Co. 89760

NOT TRANSFERABLE H.J. 117709

This coupon is issued under the authority of the
BOARD OF TRADE

1 "N" ONE UNIT

★★★

This coupon is

VALID ONLY for

the month of **JULY, 1941**

ATTENTION IS DRAWN TO THE
PROVISIONS AND CONDITIONS
APPEARING OVERLEAF

NOT TRANSFERABLE H.J. 117709

This coupon is issued under the authority of the
BOARD OF TRADE

1 "N" ONE UNIT

★★★

This coupon is

VALID ONLY for

the month of **JULY, 1941**

ATTENTION IS DRAWN TO THE
PROVISIONS AND CONDITIONS
APPEARING OVERLEAF

Petrol Ration Book for RA 1489. Two unused units inside. From when war broke out in late 1939 petrol for private use could only be bought with coupons like this for a decade, though it was not available at all from late 1942 to May 1945.

(Top) 1929 Cotton with its distinctive "Triangulated" frame. By 1929 the larger capacity Cottons had saddle tanks but the smaller Villiers engined machines retained the old style tanks fitted between the frame top tubes, a much more attractive configuration. The larger capacity machines were fitted with J.A.P or Blackburne engines.

(Bottom) My first motorcycle. A 1930 175cc Triumph two stroke with unit construction two speed gearbox. Price new £24.17.6. when introduced in mid 1930 but reduced by £1 for the Motorcycle Show. I paid £2.10.0. for mine in December 1939.

Chapter Seven
The Bike Bug Bites

So was my stay on the Abergele farm a complete waste of time? Absolutely not! I was to make a discovery that changed the course of my life. No, not girls...motorcycles!

Iorwerth had a 1929 350cc Cotton. Cottons were peculiar looking machines with their unique triangulated frame: A pair of frame tubes ran from the rear wheel spindle to the top of the steering head and a similar pair ran from the rear wheel spindle to the bottom of the steering head. This provided an immensely strong, rigid structure with the benefit of excellent handling in its day. Good handling, remember, was by no means universal in the early days and the great Stanley Woods won his first T.T. on a 350 Cotton in 1923.

In the 1920's when petrol tanks went below the frame top tube or tubes, the pencil slim Cotton petrol tanks, sloping upwards at an angle from the ground, made for a quite attractive configuration. When the larger bulbous "saddle tanks" became the fashion in the late 1920's the Cotton tanks sloping upwards and situated above the frame top tubes made for a rather ugly motorcycle.

Obviously I was very interested in the Cotton so Iorwerth told me that if I got him a gallon of petrol he would teach me to ride it. I got the petrol, put it in the tank, then Iorwerth reneged on his promise! Promises, promises...

One Sunday, however, Iorwerth was away visiting his parents so I got the machine out of its shed. The machine was not taxed or on the road and I had absolutely no idea how to start it: Amazingly, however, I got it going.

Once the engine was running I opened the right hand handlebar lever and the engine continued to run as before. This was the air lever though I had no idea at the time. Next I opened the left hand handlebar lever and the engine raced away: I quickly put it back! This, of course, was the ignition lever which *should* have been opened! As it was I ran the machine fully retarded.

I ran the machine into the large field adjoining the farm and off I went. This was marvellous! Great fun and I bumped along, changing gear with the lever on the right hand side of the tank.

Having ridden the machine round and round I was approached by two small boys from the nearby council houses who asked me to give them a ride. I pointed out that I could only take one. "No" they said: "Our dad puts one on the pillion, the other on the tank! So they climbed aboard and we happily rode round and round until my gallon of petrol ran out!

But from then on I was hooked and to own a motorcycle was an irresistible ambition.

When war broke out in September 1939 we all knew that nothing would be the same again and were apprehensive about the inevitable horrors ahead. At home a frantic rush to get Stella Maris fitted out with blackout curtains and provisions, such as sugar, bought from everywhere to help with the rationing that was sure to come.

A heady spirit of excitement filled those early days of the war and the war news and newsreels showed Hitler's relentless drive into Poland which was no match for the invincible German war machine.

After the fall of Poland, however, there was an uncanny lull: The French were secure behind their massive Maginot Line and all that appeared to be reported were "Artillery duels". The war, in fact, used to be spoken of by journalists as the "Phoney War" or even the "Bore War": They spoke too soon!

So although the War had started and both food and petrol were rationed we were not too greatly affected in those early months.

My maternal grandfather used to use "B. P. Plus" in his car, price one shilling and three halfpence (just over six pence) a gallon. When war started, however, there were no more proprietary brands and "Pool" petrol was introduced at one shilling and sixpence (seven and a half pence) a gallon. Such a huge increase in cost was considered beyond belief! Whatever was the world coming to? Who could have visualised petrol at about £3.15 a gallon today...and rising! Better read this quickly before it goes up yet again! (Sorry, petrol has just gone up 19 pence per gallon!)

Having experienced the excitement of riding that 350 Cotton, my problem was to persuade my mother to allow me to buy a motorcycle: No easy task! At last, however, she gave in and consent was obtained. Next problem was to find a machine in my price range...Fifty Bob! i.e. two pounds ten shillings (two pounds fifty pence).

Nothing in Rhyl, of course, but eventually a friend told me of a machine in Chester owned by a chap he knew. The bike was a 1930 175cc Triumph Model X two stroke, unit construction, two speed. Now this was probably Triumph's least successful model of all time, built right down to the minimum price in those lean depression years. Discussing it many years later with that legendary motorcycle rider and manufacturer of the S.O.S. motorcycle, Len Vale Onslow, he said "I owned one once and it was the worst bike I ever had!"

The owner was a young chap named Harold Slack who lived in Park Drive, Chester. The road sloped downhill, handy if you owned a 175 Triumph and the house was about halfway down on the right hand side.

A peculiarity of the Model X was that you had to declutch to kick start: The exposed kick-start quadrant engaged the exposed kick start pinion on the end of the clutch shaft: Yes, you're right...they don't make 'em like that anymore! The slightest amount of clutch drag...and there was always clutch drag...made kick starting almost impossible so few Model X's retained their kick starters: Harold's certainly hadn't!

We went to Chester by train and having eventually arrived at Park Drive, saw this lovely, desirable bike leaning against the wall. Harold then proceeded to try to start it.

Harold pushed it in gear down the road: Nothing happened! Wheeled it back up again and tried again: Still nothing! A third try...still no good!

A perspiring Harold then turned to me and said "Are you still interested?" A silly question: Wild horses wouldn't have dragged me away from there without that bike!

Eventually, having heated the plug on the gas stove, the reluctant Triumph was persuaded to start and I rode it up and down the road...marvellous! Fifty bob changed hands and I was the proud owner of WE 8238, November 1930 Sheffield registration. Afternoon tea then very kindly provided by Harold's mum. They had a goldfish pond in the garden, most unusual in those days and a guinea pig which, when released, raced round and round the living room!

Then a push to Chester station. Hard work? Not in my state of euphoria!

So I had my own motorcycle at last and the freedom of the road was mine to enjoy with the superlative Vale of Clwyd at my doorstep. Riding that 175 Triumph was a marvellous experience, everything I could have asked for and it gave me a love of motorcycles and motorcycling that I have never lost.

I recently watched a young chap getting on his machine...Just as I did at his age. I have never subscribed to the theory that young people today are in some respects a lesser breed than we were: After all, Cicero was making a similar complaint around two thousand years ago and he was wrong, too.

So what, if anything, was the difference? Well, he had a pair of L plates on his machine as I did. His machine was a scooter: Not available when I started, but a powered two wheeler just the same. He wore a full face crash helmet: Again, unknown in my day. Finally he wore a gold ear ring!

So did I envy him? Of course! He has it all ahead of him: Bikes, girls, life...the lot . Would I have changed places with him if that was possible? Of course: But I don't know about that ear ring!

Not long after I had the machine I had to take it in to the Morville garage, East Parade for repair and they diagnosed a rebore. This took ages and cost an astronomical £4. In addition the tyres were practically bald, but they had to do.

Now the trouble with Rhyl was that there were so few motorcyclists to talk to and get help or advice. I knew that the machine had to be run in at 30mph but didn't know that the engine had to be run under a light load and not strained. Perfectly obvious? Of course, but not to me then!

After the rebore I decided on a long trip to run it in so with my friend J.K.T. on the pillion off we went to Abergele, then the long climb up the hill towards Llanfair Talhaiarn. (Got it, yet? If not just Anglicise it to Lanfurter Lion!) The same hill down which I had driven those bullocks!

A mile or so up the hill and the engine seized! This, of course, was inevitable though obviously I didn't know that at the time. We let the engine cool down then pushed the bike back down the hill and it started, so off we went again heading for Denbigh. The engine tightened up once or twice but we always managed to get started again until eventually, about five miles from Denbigh, it stopped and refused to start again. A fellow motorcyclist who lived nearby did his best to help but we finally had to give up and push the bike to Denbigh. We left the machine at a garage and caught a bus back to Rhyl.

A few days later the garage managed to get the machine going and I was able to collect it.

Surely the best new motorcycle value of all time. £29.17.6. is as indelibly stamped on the memory of every 1930's motorcyclist as 1066 is stamped on every schoolboy's.

Two solemn sixteen year olds on the 1930 Triumph two stroke with a lifetime of motorcycling enjoyment ahead. I am in the top photograph, Cedryn Jones below.

Chapter Eight
The Nineteen Thirties

The dominant theme of the 1930's was the Great Depression: On Black Thursday, October 24th. 1929, a wave of panic hit the New York Stock Exchange with orders to sell "At any price" and thirteen million shares changed hands. Police Riot Squads had to be called in to attempt to disperse the panic stricken crowds on Wall Street. Eleven speculators were said to have committed suicide on the day.

But the Wall Street Crash was not merely confined to America and economies throughout the World were sucked down into the vortex. By March 1930 unemployment in Britain had soared to one and a half million, an increase of over half a million from only nine months before. By August it had rocketed to over two million.

In August 1931 the Labour Government folded and the Nation suffered its worst ever financial crisis. An all-party National Government was formed headed by the outgoing Prime Minister, Ramsay MacDonald, pledged to restore confidence in Sterling "On which the well-being of a large part of the Civilised World rests".

A month later, on September 20th, Ramsay MacDonald was forced to eat his words and devalue the pound. A massive 30% devaluation which dropped Sterling from $4.86 to the £ to $3.40 to the pound.

On October 30th. 1932 there were riots in London and other major cities protesting against unemployment and the hated "Means Test".

On November 8th. 1932 Franklin D. Roosevelt became President of the United States and promised the Nation a "New

45

Deal" with a series of far reaching measures. This was, indeed, a turning point and from then on the recession did start to ease. Within 100 days many new measures had been passed through Congress: $3 billion had been allocated to public works to stimulate the economy and, for good measure, prohibition was ended. But it was not all good news because on January 30th. 1933 Adolf Hitler became Chancellor of Germany. The rest of his Cabinet believed that they would soon tame Hitler and his wild men in brown uniforms with swastika arm bands but they were to be proved wrong! By April the boycott of Jewish businesses in Germany had begun with many shops forced to close and a wave of violence against Jews. By September there were 45,000 in Concentration Camps, including Dachau.

In November the British Government admitted that its policy of cutting arms spending in the hope that other nations would follow suit had failed. Spending on the armed forces was to be increased to bring Britain up to the standard of other Great Powers.

On September 5th. 1934 at the Nazi Party's huge Nuremburg Rally Adolf Hitler, to rapturous applause, declared that the Reich would endure for a thousand years.

In March 1935 further expansion plans were announced for the British armed forces, intended to counter Germany's rearmament and the RAF strength was to be trebled during the following three years.

On May 6th. 1935 the whole Nation celebrated King George the Fifth's Silver Jubilee but, sadly, less than a year later on January 28th. 1936 he was dead.

In October, Mussolini's troops marched into Abyssinia and in the same month Clement Attlee a "Mouse-like middle class Fabian" was elected as the "Stop-gap" leader of the Labour Party.

In February 1936 a factory was opened in Germany to produce the Volkswagen "Peoples' Car" designed by Ferdinand Porche. The objective was to motorise the masses in Germany as the Model T Ford had done in America.

In March 1936 the first Spitfire flew, designed by R.J.Mitchell and powered by the Rolls Royce Merlin engine but the power output of the new engine could not be revealed for "Defence reasons".

In May 1936 the 80,733 ton Queen Mary made her maiden voyage. The cost for the crossing to America, including all meals, was from £37 to £59.

In July, war broke out in Spain when the Army under General Franco took arms against the Republican Government and on a lighter note, the board game, Monopoly, hit America.

In August, television pictures with sound were transmitted from Alexandra Palace with Leslie Mitchell as the announcer. The new television sets were on show in the Radio Show at Olympia, expected to cost about £100. But, of course, reception would only be in the London area.

October saw the start of the "Jarrow Crusade" when 200 unemployed Jarrow men marched to London to protest against unemployment: There was an unbelievable 68% unemployment in Jarrow.

In December 1936 King Edward the Eighth abdicated to be with Mrs Simpson, "The woman I Love" and in May 1937 George the Sixth was crowned King.

In March 1938 Hitler's troops marched into Austria to scenes of wild enthusiasm and in October they marched into Czechoslovakia. The run up to World War Two had begun and the reign of terror against the Jews was intensified: All Jewish property was confiscated.

In February 1939 plans were announced to provide corrugated iron "Anderson Shelters" to householders in London and other large cities.

In May, Germany and Italy formed their political and military alliance known as the "Pact of Steel" confirming mutual support in time of war with "All military forces". A clause decreed that they "are resolved to act side by side and with united forces to secure their living space".

On September 1st 1939, Germany invaded Poland and on September 3rd at 9.15am Mr. Chamberlain sent an ultimatum to Germany. No reply was received so at 11am the German Embassy was told that a state of war now existed between the two countries. France declared war later the same day. So we were finally at war and nothing would be the same again.

On the day war was declared a German U Boat sank the British liner Athenia with the loss of 112 lives, a menacing portent of the horrors to come and by the end of the month the U Boats had claimed another 19 victims.

Churchill was brought in out of the shadows to be First Lord of the Admiralty, a post he had held a quarter of a century before.

Air Minister Kingsley Wood declared that he would refuse to bomb the Black Forest as it was private property! Air power, however, had changed out of all recognition since 1918 and before the War some experts had predicted 100,000 casualties during the first few weeks after the outbreak of war with law and order breaking down as the civilian population was overcome by panic. Vast numbers of cardboard coffins were stacked away and lime pits dug to cope with the dead.

Although the predicted carnage did not arrive, Britain was eventually to be subjected to a dreadful bombing campaign though it always failed to break civilian morale. We were, however, bombed with Wartime Regulations and Identity Cards were being prepared for everyone.

There was a rush to buy blackout curtain material as no light could be shown through windows at night. All cars had dimmed headlamps and headlamp cowls were soon to arrive: For the time being, headlamps were to be covered with cardboard with two inch wide holes and only one headlamp was allowed to be lit. Railway carriages had blue bulbs and buses were unlit. Road deaths doubled.

In early October Kapitanleutnant Gunther Prien in U Boat U47 carried out one of the most daring U Boat attacks of the war. He managed to sneak into Scapa Flow, despite its U Boat defences, to sink the Royal Oak. 400 men were saved but 800 went down with her where they lie to this day.

Gunther Prian had visited Scapa Flow as a "holidaymaker" before the War and had used this opportunity to carefully study the area with a view to the possibility of a future U Boat attack. Later in the War he and his crew were all killed in the Atlantic when the U47 was sunk by depth charges in 1941.

In October the British Expeditionary Force had landed in France and by the end of the year shipping faced a new menace: Magnetic Mines.

So that was the prelude to the 1940's. War was to ravage Europe and spread across the World. Peace was five and a half years away and many millions, on both sides, were destined never to see it.

During 1938 and 1939 my mother was worried sick at the prospect of war. Surely no-one would be able to go on holiday in wartime? In the event, of course, things were not so bad after all and the lifesaver was the Ministry of Works: They decided to evacuate to Rhyl and accommodation was required.

Mother elected to take girls and although the rate paid was low it was for 52 weeks in the year, not seasonal. So Stella Maris was full of lovely and intelligent girls. They made marvellous companions and rode many miles on the pillion of my motorcycle. Lots of light-hearted kisses, all entirely innocent: The permissive society, remember, had not been invented then!

Having abandoned the possibility of a career in farming I thought hard about the future and decided that it would have to be engineering. Although I had gained a School Certificate at Epworth I needed to upgrade it to Matriculation standard for a career in engineering and as Epworth had closed, though it was to re-open later in a different location, the option was Rhyl County School.

Now Rhyl County was a good school and Rhyl parents, in the main, were very interested in getting the best education for their children but, of course, it was entirely different from Epworth: Rhyl County took a complete cross section of society whereas Epworth was entirely middle class. The other great difference was that the County was a mixed school.

Having attended Epworth College for so long I was, naturally enough, concerned about going to Rhyl County School. What would it be like? Would the teaching staff be much inferior to that at Epworth? At Epworth everyone was keen to learn so you had no problem with unruly pupils with no intention of learning but with every intention of disrupting the class and making it difficult for others who wished to make progress. Would it be different at Rhyl County School?

In the event I had no need to worry as the standards were excellent and there were no disruptive pupils to hinder progress.

A mixed school has the great social advantage of putting boys and girls together and as they grow up together they are automatically at ease in each others' company. A single sex school, however, has the educational advantage of having no

49

distractions. Despite the delicious distractions of girls, girls, girls, however, I was able to obtain a better School Certificate up to matriculation standard.

So I am most grateful for the opportunity of attending Rhyl County School. It gave me the opportunity to upgrade my School Certificate when Epworth had closed and no complaints about the quality of teaching.

The stage was set, then, for a career in engineering and a leap into the unknown. Up until then I had enjoyed the privilege of living in a seaside town with all its advantages. What would it be like to move to a town in the industrial Midlands? Living in "digs" and working in an engineering factory was bound to be a huge culture shock, I decided: I was not to be disappointed!

More value for money: How about new batteries at four shillings
(20 pence) and leather gauntlet gloves at one shilling and
eightpence (under 10 pence).

51

(Top) Mid Thirties Morgan three-wheeler. This is the 1,000cc ohv
vee twin model. A really thrilling, bouncy ride behind that lusty,
thundering engine; but beware those diabolical brakes!
(Bottom) 1927 Douglas 350cc twin. Unusual, but handy, gear lever
through the tank top. Lovely, smooth, horizontally opposed twin
cylinder engine but, Oh, that shocking speed wobble!

Chapter Nine
The Model X and Motorcycle Matters

Now the Model X was a machine not renowned for rice pudding skin removal, nor was easy starting one of its virtues! On steeper hills it would run out of steam so you had to jump off and run alongside, hanging onto the handlebars; On local hills I became adept at jumping off at exactly the right moment!

It had a lever throttle, not a twistgrip i.e. like an air lever, but longer, on the right hand side of the handlebar near the right hand handgrip. It sounds strange today but you accepted it; in fact "twist grip" used to be a selling point in the adverts of those days.

The 175cc capacity, too, was a snag because although you paid the under 200cc insurance rate you had to pay the 150 to 250cc tax. This was twenty two shillings and sixpence a year compared to twelve shillings a year. I, of course, paid quarterly i.e. six shillings and threepence a quarter compared to three shillings and fourpence. The difference seems nothing, now, but seemed huge to me then!

Money, you will agree, is terrible stuff:

"The poor have too little, the beggar has none, the rich too much, sufficient...not one."

The trouble, of course, is that you can't do a darned thing without it!.

In the 1930's we were always being told that "Money doesn't matter." George Bernard Shaw argued that it must be immensely important, otherwise why was so much effort expended in telling us all that it didn't matter when the mass of the people had so little of it anyway? Nowadays, of course, that "money doesn't matter" argument is stone dead, as obsolete as the dinosaurs!

Samuel Johnson had it right a couple of centuries ago when he wrote:

"In modern society money will serve you better than principles. Sir, you may make the experiment: Go out into the street and give one man a lecture on morality and another a shilling and see which will respect you most".

Nothing has changed....except the purchasing power of that shilling!

Perhaps this is a good moment to explain the old pounds shillings and pence system: There were twenty shillings in a pound and twelve pence in a shilling. As a shilling was a twentieth of a pound it was equivalent to five new pence. A penny was a twelfth of that i.e. just under half a new penny. Slang term for a shilling was a "bob" and sixpence was a "tanner". Standard slang terms for sums often used to buy motorcycles were "fifty bob" i.e. two pounds fifty pence today, or a "fiver". Still in use, of course. "Ten bob" translated to fifty pence today. Got it? Clear as mud!

Inflation has made a nonsense of money and our whole understanding of it and as prices are so often mentioned in this narrative, it might be a good idea to outline how the value of money has changed...for the worse!

My landlord, Joe Randle, had served his apprenticeship in a small engineering firm in Derby before W.W. One. At the end of the week his boss used to say "£20 gone and only nineteen men paid!" That, of course, was before my time but let us look at inflation from 1939.

Between 1939 and post war, say 1947, my own estimate is that inflation was somewhere between two and three hundred percent. For the period 1947 to 1997 we have the "benefit" of official figures during which the cost of living index increased twenty fold. This, however, does not give the complete picture: Petrol in 1947 was about two shillings a gallon i.e. one tenth of a pound. Now in 1999 it is about £3.15 per gallon i.e. over thirty times the 1947 value. Tax on a gallon of petrol in 1947 was ninepence (under 4 pence). Now it is £2.44, over sixty times the 1947 figure. (and Petrol has just been increased by an extra 19 pence per gallon.)

House price inflation, however, is far higher than the official twenty times 1947 values. A £2,000 house in 1947 would probably be worth £200,000 today i.e. 100 times 1947 value. These figures are mine, not "official", but I would have thought that whatever basis was used you would still arrive at a multiple of not less than seventy five times value for executive houses.

To live through, and cope with, a period of inflation of such magnitude has been quite an experience especially as inflation is by no means dead! But, for the moment, back to 1939 and the fifty bob Model X Triumph.

So what *had* the Model X got in its favour? Well it did provide me with a marvellous measure of mobility, enabling me to explore the magnificent North Wales countryside and longer journeys, too. For such a bread and butter model the frame design was excellent, far ahead of many of its rivals. Twin frame tubes ran from the rear wheel spindle to either side of the steering head to which they were brazed. They then continued down in front of the engine, under the engine and back to the rear wheel spindle. The engine sat securely in this excellent cradle and the triangular tank with its rounded front sat below the twin top tubes. This frame design was very similar to the later, highly regarded, S.O.S. machines, though their frames were all welded: A unique system in its day.

So the little Triumph handled very well indeed and was a joy to swing round the bends and that, after all, is what motorcycling is all about. Maximum speed was, I suppose, about 40/45 M.P.H. though no speedometer was fitted: Not a legal requirement in those days. Flat out you felt you were doing "The ton".

Having bought the Model X the first problem was insurance and I quickly found out that conventional insurance companies just do not want to insure motorcycles. Best quote locally was £5 and the bike had cost half that. I finally got fixed up for £3.10. with a broker who advertised in "The Motor Cycle" from Honiton, Devon.

I would have loved to have owned a 150cc overhead valve machine and my ambition was a 150 New Imperial. There was a long neglected one that stood leaning against a wall, visible from the road, at some premises at the foot of the H bridge. I stood and looked at it enviously often enough but never dared ask about it!

I bought one eventually, almost half a century later and riding it was an experience I would not have missed. So would I have been the happiest youngster in Britain if I had owned one at sixteen? Yes, I'm sure I would!.

After machines of today I was surprised at the high gearing and low revving engine but delighted with the crisp bark of the exhaust: A remarkable machine for its day.

The spurt in design for the 150cc class was caused by the announcement in the 1932 Budget of a new tax rate for machines of under 150cc. Up to that date all machines up to 250cc were taxed at the same rate. Designers rushed to their drawing boards and produced new models for the 1932 Motorcycle Show ready for the 1933 season.

Many used the easily available Villiers engines but the more adventurous designed new O.H. valvers. These small overhead valve machines showed the way design was to go and were the forerunners of today's Honda 50's. They were, of course, handicapped by the petrol of the day which was only about 65 octane, compared to about 100 octane today. (The huge engines in World War One tanks had to make do with 45 octane and needed three men on the starting handle, but I digress!)

By 1939, however, the 150cc Royal Enfields could bat along at 60 MPH... remarkable going for those days. The O.H.V. Triumphs and BSA's were short lived with the Triumphs only being produced for 1933/4 but they were, in my opinion, the prettiest lightweights of their day, using the excellent frame design of the Model X, though now with a fashionable saddle tank covering the frame top tubes. Three speed hand change gearbox, too. It took a further twenty years for Triumphs to produce another 150 overhead valve machine, the Terrier, soon to be uprated to the 200cc Tiger Cub.

Then, of course, there was the question of motorcycle clothing. Once again "The Motor Cycle" was consulted and Pride and Clarke's adverts carefully studied. Pride and Clarke sold all kinds of motorcycle accessories from clothing to motor oil at fifteen shillings for five gallons.

A rubberised motorcycle coat was selected at twelve shillings, a pair of leather gauntlet gloves at one and eightpence and a close fitting leather helmet like a flying helmet at two shillings. Crash helmets were only used in competition then, not on the road. A pair of goggles at sixpence completed the outfit.

Petrol, of course, was rationed: two gallons a month for under 250cc and three gallons a month for larger capacities: Not a lot for a new motorcyclist, keen to explore the roads and lanes of the Vale of Clwyd. An old school friend, however, George Brookes of Cwybr Farm, Rhuddlan Road, Rhyl used to very kindly let me have the odd gallon and this was a great help.

Iorwerth used to leave his motorcycle in the yard at Stella Maris when he came to Rhyl in the evenings. It had the dual advantage of safe parking and the opportunity to chat up the girls who worked at Stella Maris.

He must have sold the Cotton because he never appeared on it. He did, however, come on a 1927 350cc twin cylinder Douglas which was in very good order despite being an old bike. When he was out on the town I decided to have a ride on it and was very impressed by the smoothness of the twin cylinder engine. There was no point in asking his permission as he would have said "No"! The three speed gearbox was operated by a lever that came through the top of the flat tank.

I opened it up on the Rhuddlan Road and when the speed built up it went into a speed wobble, my first experience of this remarkable phenomenon.

The front wheel whipped from side to side and no amount of force on the handlebars could restrain it. Goodness knows how I got out of it and stayed on the machine but I was told, later, that you should accelerate *through* it and then slow down. It would, however, take a very brave man who could keep the throttle open under those conditions and I had a dreadful fright.

They do not, thank goodness, build bikes that go into speed wobbles these days!

That Douglas speed wobble was the worst I have ever experienced but years later, on a 350 Tiger 80 Triumph, a similar thing happened. With one hand off the handlebars to adjust my goggles I hit a pothole at about 50 M.P.H. which threw the front wheel into a lock to lock wobble. Again, with good fortune, I managed to stay on the machine and no harm was done.

At a later date, Iorwerth turned up on a 1937 350 B.S.A. a much more modern machine. Overhead valve engine and four speed foot change gearbox .. what luxury! I sampled this, too, in his absence, and found it an excellent machine.

During the 1930's there were a number of attempts to produce an enclosed motorcycle that you could hose down to clean and that would provide a measure of weather protection. The most successful of all was the 250cc Francis Barnett "Cruiser". They were powered by 250cc Villiers engines, four speed hand change gearboxes at first but four speed foot change by the late 1930's. I did have the opportunity of riding one up and down Rhyl promenade and found it to be a delightful machine. Never owned one in their day but acquired one many years later.

Another member of the scarce motorcycle fraternity of the time was a young chap of about twenty one with a 1934 Morgan three wheeler powered by a 1,000 cc J.A.P. water cooled side valve engine. J.A.P. in those days meant J.A. Prestwich, the motorcycle engine manufacturers of Tottenham, London. Nowadays Jap means Japanese!

He was well spoken, well educated and had served an apprenticeship at Metropolitan Vickers (Metro-Vic). What he was doing in North Wales at that time, apparently with time on his hands, I don't know. He didn't live in Rhyl but further down the coast at, I believe, Colwyn Bay. Cannot remember his name but as a fellow motorcycle enthusiast who had owned many motorcycles he was a frequent caller at Stella Maris. Oddly enough I never visited his home or knew exactly where he lived.

He was, of course, an engineer and had drilled the inlet pipe of his Morgan and from it ran a rubber tube to the dashboard, sealed by a small conical wooden plug. When the engine was hot he would remove the wooden plug thus allowing in extra air and reducing fuel consumption. In those days of petrol rationing every economy was a help and this D.I.Y. dodge seemed to work.

He used to drive the Morgan with great elan and I thoroughly enjoyed being his passenger as he thundered along those country roads. He allowed me to try driving the Morgan: "Just set the throttle at a fast tickover and let the clutch in gently", he said, and away we went!

The sheer lusty power of those vee-twin engines was a remarkable experience. You couldn't have a foot controlled throttle on a Morgan as they bounced about so much: The throttle was operated by a long lever on one of the spokes of the steering wheel i.e.. like a long air or ignition lever on a motorcycle.

It was not possible to start the engine with the self starter from cold and you had to use the starting handle. In fact I cannot remember the engine being willing to start on the starter even when hot and using the exhaust valve lifter.

When a customer complained to Ettore Bugatti about the poor brakes on Bugatti cars, the "Le Patron" is reputed to have replied "I build my cars to go, not to stop!" Mr. Morgan could, with absolute accuracy, have said the same thing because Morgan brakes of that era were truly diabolical!.

By the end of the 1930's Morgan had introduced their "Four-four" four wheeler and they were to remain virtually unchanged, until 1950. You may consider Morgans old fashioned but not only have they survived but they are now Britain's only surviving independent car manufacturer.

A young chap who did sell the odd motorcycle was Jack Hughes, the nephew of Mr. Shirley of the Shirley cycle business, Vale Road, Rhyl. They had an old single storey stone built building adjoining "The Cut", a small stream that crossed under Vale Road not far from Tyn Rhyl, Rhyl's oldest house.

Mr. Shirley was an old timer and a very pleasant chap, as was his nephew, Jack. I used to enjoy chatting to Mr. Shirley about his motorcycle days.

In the 1920's a visitor to Rhyl had arrived on a motorcycle powered by a Barr and Stroud sleeve valve engine. Sleeve valve engines were perfectly successful in the aero engine field right to the end of the piston engine era but the Barr and Stroud sleeve valve engines did not have the benefit of such sustained development. The sleeve oscillated inside the cylinder and simply relied on splash lubrication, administered by a hand pump on the tank, injecting a shot of oil into the crankcase every few miles. Considering such a primitive form of lubrication, then, the Barr and Strouds did well to survive successfully.

The one that had ended up in Mr. Shirley's hands had seized and he had bought it from the owner. He stripped and carefully re-assembled it, claiming that the position of the sleeve was critical "to the width of a cigarette paper". He got it absolutely right and on re-assembly it ran with no further trouble.

Although he had long since broken up the machine he had retained the engine and half a century later I met Jack Hughes again and asked if he remembered the engine. He not only remembered it but told me he had made a motorcycle frame to take it many years later as Shirley's made their own frames in those days. It appears, however, that despite this enterprise the engine never got back on the road again.

Jack, however, as far as I know, still runs the descendant of Shirley's Cycles, now a modern shop in Queen Street, Rhyl.

(Top) In the ultimately elusive attempt to secure the Holy Grail of motorcycling, the machine for everyman, none came closer than the 250cc Francis Barnett Cruiser powered by the 250cc Villiers engine. The objective was a machine that could be hosed down like a car and with built in legshields to provide a measure of weather protection.
(Left) This was Coventry Eagle's attempt at the everyman market with a machine you could hose down. It also had the enormous advantage of a spring frame but it never challenged the Francis Barnett's mastery of that market. It also used 250 Villiers engines but some had the unusual 250cc ohv Blackburne engine.

(Top) The Austin Seven really did bring motoring for everyman. A large car in miniature under nine feet long and under four feet wide, taking up little more room than a motorcycle combination. Nothing cheap or shoddy about them and many were destined to go on for 200,000 miles or more. 750cc sidevalve four-cylinder engine. This is a 1923 "Chummy", similar to Stan's 1927 model.
(Bottom) Before World War One when most machines were single gear belt drive, Zeniths managed a limited range of gear ratios by opening and closing the engine shaft pulley enabling the drive belt to operate on a variable diameter. To make this possible the rear wheel had to be brought forwards and backwards to suit. These two movements in unison were achieved by operating a "coffee grinder" handle above the tank top.

...er Ten

...ed Engineer

...s faced the back of a house in Edward ...Stan Hughes, his wife and son, Trevor, ...out my age and was a friend throughout my

...orn engineer of remarkable versatility who worked ...chanic at Nelson Brothers Sports shop in Queen Street, ...At one time Nelsons had sold motorcycles but by the late ...50's they only sold Scott Cyc-autos: Single gear mopeds at 19 guineas, a price far beyond we youngsters though we looked at them through the shop window and dreamed! How wonderful it would be to own such a marvellous machine, propelled by an engine so no more pedalling.....bliss!

Stan was an apprentice trained engineer before World War One; seven years apprenticeship in those days, and had been a motorcycle enthusiast in his youth. One of his favourite machines was a 1,000cc Zenith Gradua on which a "coffee grinder" handle above the tank top gave a limited range of gear ratios by opening and closing the drive pulley on the engine drive-shaft and at the same time moving the rear wheel backwards and forwards to maintain belt tension.

This sounds a strange arrangement today but in the days when their opponents only had single gear belt drive it gave them a worth-while advantage. So much so, in fact, that Zenith Graduas were barred from competing against single geared machines. Zeniths turned this to their advantage by adopting the slogan "Barred" featuring a transfer of a five barred gate on their petrol tanks. Zeniths used J.A.P engines of various sizes but their most famous models had the big 1,000cc side valve vee twins.

Stan had a 1927 Austin Seven "Chummy" i.e. like the earliest 1923 model with a fold down hood. These tiny little cars were a milestone in motoring history: Many ultra light cars or cyclecars had been made but most were flimsy contraptions powered by a motorcycle engine and were destined to fail.

The Austin Seven, however, was a large car in miniature, under nine feet long and under four feet wide it was, nevertheless, a real motorcar with a 700cc, though soon uprated to 750cc, side valve four cylinder engine and, startling for the time, four wheel brakes. At the time of its introduction in 1923, front wheel brakes were considered to be dangerous so Austin had the rear wheel brakes foot pedal operated but the front brakes were operated by the hand brake to give the driver greater feel of the road conditions.

The brakes were half crown size: Sorry, gentle reader, unless you are of a certain age you will never have seen a half crown, so let's settle for minuscule. (Come to think of it, how did everyone compare the size of hailstones before golf balls were invented!). Not that the brakes were very effective, in fact someone claimed that the brakes required written notice for an emergency stop, but the thought was there!

In any event it was in good company: No doubt Herbert Austin shared Ettore Bugatti's views on brakes!

Herbert Austin laid out the design on the billiard table of his country house in the Lickey Hills near Birmingham and his objective was a car that although a four seater would take up little more room than a motorcycle combination.

At £225 when a motorcycle combination could cost £160 to £200, this was competition indeed and, worse still for the motorcycle movement, it was soon reduced to an incredible £165. When they became available second-hand and the prices were much lower, the competition really intensified.

Between 1922 and 1939 there were over 300 variants and over 300,000 were sold, giving thousands of people their introduction to motoring. They were by no means cheap and shoddy: They were built to give simple, inexpensive transport with minimum running costs together with ease of repair. Many covered 200,000 miles or more and were still running as bread and butter transport long after the War.

In the 1930's many marginal motorists would only tax their cars for two quarters i.e. April to June and July to September. The car would then be laid up for the winter months. Some motorcyclists did the same, of course. Stan's Austin Seven, however, had very little use and I am sure it was only taxed for one quarter, in the autumn, when Stan and family would go for a week's holiday to a relative near Birmingham. To avoid what little traffic there was in those days, Stan would travel at night!

Stan kept his car, nicknamed "Bunny" until after the War when T bought it for £25. Despite having been laid up throughout the War it started up with no trouble and ran just as well as before.

Stan was a very useful source of information and he put me in touch with Bill Greening, or Bill Greenin' as Stan always called him. Bill Greening lived further along the promenade. His wife ran the boarding house and Bill ran his garage business from his garage behind the house. The garage was always packed solid with cars, so closely that it would have made a sardine manufacturer green with envy. How Bill ever found the space to actually work on a car remained an unsolved mystery but Bill managed it somehow.

Bill was very helpful indeed to a tyro motorcyclist and never ran out of patience. He and Stan always had a fag in their mouths and they had mastered the energy saving art of never having to remove it between puffs: With the fag stuck to their lower lips it bounced about like a demented Jack in the Box! Stan was an inveterate collector and his workshop was a treasure trove of long abandoned machinery of all kinds. I remember an American Elto Quad outboard engine : A water cooled four-cylinder, two-stroke with a water jacket cracked by frost. Stan was going to repair it but, like so many of his potential projects, it never got done.

A fascinating survival was a World war One Rolls Royce "Hawk" aero engine. This was an in-line six cylinder engine. Designed in 1915 they eventually produced 100hp at 1,500rpm. Originally intended for training aircraft, some were fitted to Avro 504F's, but their main use was in airships for submarine spotting in the North Sea and of 55,700 hours flown by British airships during the War, no less than 36,000 hours were in Hawk engined craft.

Do not make the mistake of thinking that these engines were primitive, unreliable monstrosities: Flights of 30/35 hours were commonplace and in August 1918 a flight of 50 hours 55 minutes was recorded. Stan's intention was to fit the Hawk into a motor boat but, once again, this ambition was never realised.

At Rhyl County School I met another motorcycle fan, Cedryn Jones. Cedryn lived at Wygfair, Pendyffryn Road, Rhyl. No motorcycle at the time though he was eventually to become a true enthusiast, buying a 350cc B.S.A. B.31 immediately after the War and ending up with BMW's and large four cylinder Japanese machines. In these early days, however, we would happily work on the Model X in the garden shed at Wygfair.

Again during my trips I stopped for petrol at a corrugated iron garage at Gronant: Still there as far as I know. They had for sale a 1927 350cc side-valve James at three pounds ten shillings. The garage was owned by two brothers from Liverpool and one of them started up the James for me. He ran it at high revs in the gloomy garage until the exhaust pipe glowed dull red! Couldn't have done it much good!

Another potential enthusiast I met at that time was a young chap who had come to Rhyl with the Ministry of Works. Can't remember his name but it was Irish and, I believe, Dooley. He wanted a modestly priced bike so I had an idea!

My uncle Joe Utting, my mother's brother, had explained a theory to me: Now was the time to put it into practice! The theory was this: Someone has an article for sale at £x. You say to him "Look! If I can find you a customer at a higher price, will you split the difference with me 50/50?" He will usually agree.

I approached the Liverpool brothers with my theory and they agreed to split anything over £3.10s with me 50/50. Next to tell my pal about it, price £5. From my description he thought it would suit him so off we went on my Model X.

The bike was demonstrated, he liked it, £5 was paid and I was given fifteen shillings.. a worth while sum in those days and my first profit on a motorcycle. The James was not taxed or insured so I towed him back to Rhyl with my Triumph.

At the start of the War all signposts were removed to hinder any foreign army in the event of invasion. In addition, at the approaches to towns, huge concrete pipes were upended and placed in two diagonal rows to form a barrier about five feet high so that an invading army would be obstructed.

Coming into Rhyl from Rhuddlan there is a dip in the road and these barriers were placed well down the dip. My pal was delighted with the James and one day he took me a ride on the pillion. We were hurtling along from Rhuddlan, approaching the barrier, when his foot must have slipped off the brake and we slammed straight into the concrete pipes!

We both flew over the top and landed on the road on the far side. I was lucky, escaping with cuts and bruises but he broke an arm!

The Civil Service had their own small nursing home opposite the Palace Hotel, East Parade and I used to visit him there where he was very comfortable indeed. Pretty nurse, too!

He introduced me to the works of Sigmund Freud, telling me that once you started one of Freud's books to stick at it and not put it down, otherwise you would never finish it. Good advice! I particularly remember "Totem and Taboo": Hard going! Did they teach me anything? A little, perhaps!

He had a colleague who owned a 1937 250 Panther... how we envied him!

A favourite evening run of mine was Rhyl to St. Asaph, up the High Street hill then right via Trefnant to Denbigh. Back on the low road with an exhilarating downhill swoop over Pont yr allt Goch before St. Asaph then back to Rhyl.

At Trefnant there was a part time motorcycle repairer and dealer who lived in a council house just off the main road. He worked in a tiny garden shed in which he carried out his repairs. The bench was always piled high with motorcycle parts so how he managed to actually work on an engine defied belief!

He, too, was a very pleasant person and although extremely busy he always made time to impart information to an impecunious motorcyclist. I bought from him a 1926 350 side-valve Royal Enfield for ten shillings (50 pence). He kept the beaded edge tyres, no doubt worth more than the machine, but this was no problem for me as I had no intention to ride it on the road as tax and insurance would have been prohibitively expensive.

I bought it to increase my knowledge about motorcycles and the engine ran well and sounded well. In my search for knowledge I dismantled the engine and then managed to put it together again. When it came to valve timing, however, I hadn't a clue as I had no idea that the pinions were stamped and it was only a question of matching them up.

I resorted to trying the pinions in different positions until it sounded right i.e. it sucked on the inlet stroke and blew on the exhaust stroke. It must have been something like right because, once again, it started well, ran well and sounded well. I eventually donated it to the local Air Training Corps and, yes, it had taught me something.

In the Spring I was able to travel further afield on my motorcycle, beyond the Vale of Clwyd and into the Berwyn mountains: Lovely country again, but of different character. One memorable trip was to Anglesey, a long haul for me then. At Beaumaris I saw a Scott for the first time, parked in brilliant sunshine against the green with its companion, an International Norton.

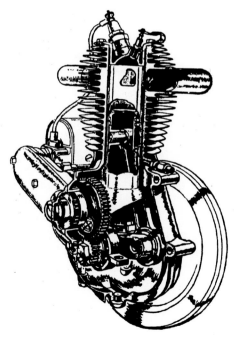

(Left) Barr and Stroud 350cc sleeve-valve engine early 1920's. Sleeve-valve engines continued successfully for decades in the aero engine field but they had the benefit of sustained development. The Barr and Stroud had to manage with a hand pump in the tank top administering a slug of oil every few miles. Even so, they were quite successful and were fitted as a proprietary engine to a number of makes, but they failed to survive the 1920's.

(Top) James 350cc side-valve 1920's. This is very like the 1927 model I sold to make my first profit on a motorcycle. Note the long, ugly gearchange lever and vertical cylinder head finning. The price was £5 and my commission was fifteen shillings (75 pence). Doesn't sound much now, but a welcome profit for a sixteen year old then.

(Top) Perchance to dream, early eighteen hundreds. One of the first ideas for a motorcycle, but there was a long way to go! (Bottom) The dream is becoming reality at last. It was not until the arrival of the internal combustion engine that successful motorcycles could evolve, but before this many inventors experimented with steam driven motorcycles. This is a Michaux "boneshaker", the first commercially successful pedal cycle in which a small Perreaux steam engine was fitted in 1869. It undoubtedly worked, though it was never developed commercially. It is preserved in France.

Chapter Eleven
First Long Run on the Triumph

At Easter I embarked on my most ambitious journey to date: To Derby, then Bridgnorth then back to Rhyl. No signposts, of course, so guided by a "Hovis" road map I headed out of Rhyl. The route was along the coast road through Flint, then on to Chester. Then Tarporley, Nantwich, Stone, Uttoxeter, Derby. I have traversed that journey many times since in every season of the year and in every kind of weather: Sunshine, rain, snow, hail, sleet, ice, flood and fog. If I have missed anything out, don't worry, I hit it anyway!

The journey went well, I managed to find my way and the Triumph gave no trouble but, oh, it was cold! A few miles before Stone there was a small group of trees at the side of the road and some workmen had a bonfire going so I stopped to get warm. They had a galvanised bucket on the fire, filled with water and when it was boiling they threw in handfuls of a mixture of tea and sugar! All new to me! The tea was then poured into mugs and they very kindly gave me one: I had never tasted better tea...marvellous! Warmed and refreshed I was ready to resume my journey.

During the Summer holidays of 1938 I had met a young chap of my own age at Cockliffe Hill Farm, Nottinghamshire, between Nottingham and Mansfield. His name was Jack and I was to stay with him and his family in Derby. They had a very pleasant house on Chellaston Road, Derby. His father worked at Rolls Royce and his mother had a small shop opposite to the entrance to Rolls Royce in Nightingale Road.

Jack had a sister, a lovely girl who was courting a young Rolls Royce apprentice named Peter Watson. I had just completed my journey and had arrived at the Nightingale Road shop when Peter Watson arrived. Of course I had never met him before and his opening words to me were: "Did you ride one hundred miles on that motorcycle?" Yes" I replied, chest swelling with pride. "I wouldn't ride a hundred yards on it" said Peter.

Not a remark calculated to win friends and influence people and I justifiably took an instant dislike to him. Now first impressions can often be absolutely mistaken but in this case subsequent acquaintance gave me no reason to change my mind!

Towards the end of his life Charlie Chester, the much loved comedian, said: "I have never met a man or woman I didn't want to like, but some of them won't let you." A statement with which I entirely agree.

A pleasant few days with Jack and his family then the trip to Bridgnorth where I was to stay with Gladys Insull and her husband. Gladys had worked for my mother for several years when I was only four or five and we never lost touch until her death in 1996.

Gladys had not married until late in life and then to a widower who was considerably older. They had a small grocer's shop at the sharp corner near the top of Cartway, Bridgnorth. Cartway was an incredibly steep road and at one time the only way from High-town to Low-town, Bridgnorth. My wife, Edna, remembers going up Cartway in her father's "Flatnose" Morris and having to leap out of the dickey seat to wedge a piece of wood under the back wheel to stop the car rolling backwards when it had panted to a standstill. The piece of wood was always kept ready to hand for such emergencies!

In the nineteen thirties, however, a new road was built on the other side of town with a much more gradual slope but the old Cartway had been a fearsome obstacle for early motorists and, of course, horses and carts.

During my stay at Bridgnorth my trusty steed once again proved impossible to start, despite pushing it in gear down Cartway. I took it to Foxalls, the local garage and collected it a few days later.

The mechanic told me that "The Boss" had decided that in his opinion the gearbox was not adequately lubricated so he had put gear oil into it and the bike was now running. With hindsight, of course, I now know what was wrong with the machine then and the reasons for the earlier seizures on the Abergele/Denbigh run: The piston rings would partially seize and stick in their grooves. If you had taken out the plug, put in a tablespoonful of oil and rotated the engine with the plug OUT this would have given a temporary seal. Sparking plug was replaced and the machine would have started and continued to run.

The simple two speed gearbox on the Model X was perfectly adequately lubricated by petroil. The oil the garage had put in, however, had splashed about under the piston and had created the temporary seal which was good enough to get the engine going again.

Do remember this dodge when your two-stroke chain saw, hedge trimmer, lawn mower or any other two-stroke engine will not start when hot. On these smaller engines a teaspoonful of oil will do the trick and we use it to this day. Take the sparking plug out, put in the oil and rotate the engine a few times to thoroughly coat the piston rings with oil. Replace the plug and the engine should start.

On the Model X this was the last time I experienced this trouble: Eventually the piston and rings bedded in to provide an adequate seal and the bike was to travel many miles in my hands. The run back to Rhyl was again enjoyable and trouble free so I arrived home delighted to have completed this marathon round trip.

At the outbreak of war the camps round Rhyl filled with soldiers and the Royal Corps of Signals was based at Kinmel Camp which had also been an important army base in the first World War: So Rhyl, for once, was crowded in winter as well as summer.

The winter of 1939/40 was bitterly cold and even Rhyl did not escape but the cold weather did not deter me from riding my motorcycle. Protected by my Pride and Clarke riding gear and thick scarf, knitted by one of the girls staying at Stella Maris I was ready to battle with the elements.

The war news was as before with "Artillery duels" as the highlights but when Spring came, everything changed: For the first time we knew the meaning of "Blitzkrieg", Lightning War.

The Germans ignored the Maginot Line and simply swept through Belgium, as they had in World War One. The War was frighteningly close at last and the newsreels showed screaming Stukas machine gunning the French roads, choked with refugees.

The irresistible German armies raced through France and then came Dunkirk. In Rhyl soldiers flooded in from Dunkirk in all kinds of ragged and makeshift clothing. The War really was on our doorstep.

In a bewilderingly short time, France had fallen, we were driven out of mainland Europe with only that narrow strip of water, the English Channel, to save us from invasion.

From then on embattled Britain stood alone against the mighty German war machine. Had Hitler chosen to invade then, with the facilities to do it, the War would surely have been lost. He failed to do so and put his faith into an all out air attack against Britain. This was to last all through the summer and it became to be known as "The Battle of Britain".

The U-boats, too, entered their killing fields and the "Grey Wolves" mounted an all out offensive against allied shipping.

This posed a potentially fatal strike against Britain as with supplies cut off, the nation would be starved into submission but once again, as in World War One, the convoy system was to save the day though it was "A damned close run thing".

For me in Rhyl, however, that period up to leaving school at the end of the Summer term was my last opportunity to enjoy a very pleasant way of life. The pleasure of riding my motorcycle through delightful countryside, the enjoyment of Rhyl in holiday mood again and a pretty girl at my side on a park bench to watch the moonlight glittering on the waters of the Marine Lake.

So at last the time came to leave Rhyl and end forever the enjoyable life there. Leave behind, too, the lovely girls who lived at Stella Maris...Pat, Rosalind, Moira, Moyna, Isabel (who lived "somewhere near Inverness", though I never knew exactly where), Sally, Joyce, Mary, Pam and many others, not forgetting Mildred Howley.

Now if Sam Goldwyn was looking for a stage name for his newest star, Mildred Howley is not a name that would have sprung immediately to mind, yet Mildred, despite a name reminiscent of an elderly schoolmarm, was breathtakingly beautiful. So did she ever ride on the pillion of my motorcycle and share carefree kisses? Sadly, no, as I never plucked up enough courage to ask this delectable creature. They were a wonderful crowd of girls: Witty, intelligent, attractive...I was going to miss them.

So on my bike to Derby and the new, grim, world of work. I was to know every inch of that road both ways in every kind of weather and in every season of the year.

From Rhyl you head for Chester either by the top road or the bottom road. The Model X liked the bottom road best as it was flat: You go through Prestatyn, Gronant, then along the side of the Dee estuary through Ffonengrew, Mostyn, Hollywell, Flint then Chester. When we graduated to more powerful machines we preferred the top road: Dyserth, over the mountain to the top of Hollywell, Hawaden, then down onto the Cheshire Plain to Chester. Total mileage just over thirty.

From Chester a run through pleasant Cheshire countryside to Tarvin, Tarporley, Nantwich, just over 20 miles. Then another twenty miles or so of very attractive rolling country through Woore, Pipegate and on to Stone. From Stone a hilly minor road to Uttoxeter, about twelve miles, then the eighteen miles of level farmland through Sudbury and Etwall to Derby, total one hundred and five miles.

A very pleasant road for motorcycling with hills and bends to provide plenty of interest and lovely country all the way.

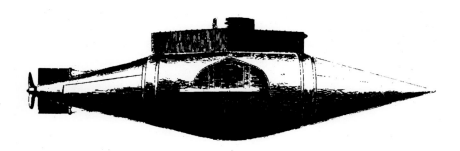

(Top) This is a Bleriot monoplane similar to Vivian Hewitt's. He was the first person to fly the Irish Sea in 1911. Starting from Rhyl he flew to Anglesey then flew the 64 miles to Dublin, a greater distance across water than anyone had flown before, and without a compass!

(Bottom) The Resurgam (I shall rise again) probably the world's first mechanically driven submarine. Towed out of Rhyl harbour on 24th February 1880 en route to Portsmouth for evaluation by the Admiralty, the towline broke and she sank off Rhyl where she lies to this day.

Chapter Twelve
Above, Below and On the Waves at Rhyl

Strange as it may seem, Rhyl does have a connection with the early days of aviation via Vivian Hewitt. His family were members of the "Beerage", the wealthy people who made their money out of brewing and whose fortunes continued on to future generations. The family business was Hewitt Brothers, Tower Brewery, Grimsby. The beauty of the brewery business is that in good times people drink to celebrate and in hard times they drink to cheer themselves up!

Vivian's father was not interested in the brewing business and was content with his income of £8,000 per annum from the brewery, equivalent to about half a million today. He bought an estate at Bodfari, in the Vale of Clwyd, a few miles from Rhyl.

His son, Vivian, was always interested in mechanics and after his education at Harrow he went to serve his apprenticeship at the railway workshops in Crewe. His apprenticeship completed he then rented a shed at Brooklands in 1909 where he raced cars and pursued his interest in aviation.

His first aeroplane was an Antoinette, a gift from his Uncle Tom from Grimsby, but such was its low power output that to judge when conditions were suitable for flying you lit a match in the open air: If it burned out completely without enough air movement to blow it out, then it was safe to fly!

His next aeroplane was another gift from Uncle Tom, a Bleriot monoplane with a five cylinder 25hp Rhone rotary engine. Vivian was to say later that they were the weakest twenty five horses in all creation!

Forecasting in 1912, Vivian claimed that the very presence of aircraft in the skies would result in the end of all war. What a pity that this forecast was so woefully wide of the mark!

In 1911 he bought his third aeroplane, another Bleriot, but this time with a 50 hp Gnome rotary engine and with this aircraft he determined to attempt the first aeroplane crossing of the Irish Sea.

He then moved from Bodfari to Rhyl, setting up a hangar and airfield on the other side of the River Clwyd at Kinmel Bay and on October 1911 he made the first ever aeroplane flight over Rhyl.

For his attempt on the crossing of the Irish Sea he started out from Rhyl, heading for Holyhead where the distance to Dublin is 60 miles, a greater distance over water than anyone had ever flown before. The actor and keen aviation enthusiast Robert Loraine, however, had almost made it eighteen months before when his Antoinette started from Anglesey but landed in the sea a mile or two off the Irish coast.

For the 60 mile crossing, Vivian Hewitt had no compass......a piece of equipment you might well have thought indispensable, especially as three previous airmen had been lost when making the attempt! During the flight he ran into a bank of fog but beforehand he had memorised the shadow of the sun on his wings so that when he came out of the fog he adjusted his direction of flight to put the shadow back in approximately the same place and carried on! You can well understand that he found it a "great relief" when he eventually sighted land.

He continued on to land at Phoenix Park, Dublin and the record was established. The Dublin papers reporting the flight also carried an advertisement announcing Robert Loraine at the Gaiety Theatre, Dublin in George Bernard Shaw's "Man and Superman".

Robert Loraine was to command No 40 Squadron on the Western Front in which Mick Mannock scored his first victory. Mannock was to become Britain's highest scoring pilot, credited with 73 victories. A fellow member of No 40 Squadron, flying with Mannock at the time and who witnessed his victory was L.B.Blaxland. He had Derbyshire connections because he was later to teach at Repton and finally became the Vicar of Doveridge near Uttoxeter. Lionel Blaxland not only fought the Richthofen Circus but also had the doubtful distinction of landing his Sopwith

Pup on Southend Pier after an engine failure and, for good measure, fusing the electric railway!

At the outbreak of War Vivian Hewitt immediately volunteered and was sent to Farnborough to test aeroplanes. He also presented the Government with a £50,000 loan, interest free, to be repaid at the end of the War.

Vivian Hewitt never married and later moved to Anglesey taking with him his housekeeper from Rhyl and her husband. He lived in an isolated house, surrounded by a high wall, with no electricity or running water. He was an inveterate collector and his favourite reading appeared to be my "Club Magazine", the "Exchange and Mart"! He would buy every kind of equipment, unpack it with great care and then, with equal care, we re-pack it where it would remain, never to see the light of day again.

Like many immensely wealthy men he was paranoid about paying tax and eventually emigrated to the Bahamas.

Another first for Rhyl was the "Resurgam".. meaning "I will rise again". The Resurgam was the world's first power driven submarine. The chief problems that faced early submarine builders were firstly, how to maintain enough air to breathe when the craft was submerged and secondly, how to propel it under water.

Her inventor, George William Garrett, a curate, believe it or not, invented a chemical air purifier and using it he managed to remain submerged for 45 minutes in the River Seine.

A single cylinder steam engine provided the power but how to use it when submerged? The answer was to store high pressure steam in a very strong insulated boiler so that the steam could be gradually released to power the engine. This system was supposed to keep the submarine going for hours under water but I must say that this seems optimistic!

The cigar shaped Resurgam was built at Birkenhead and launched on December 10th 1879. It was claimed that it remained submerged for 30 hours, with the three man crew standing in stifling heat, but this length of time seems "remarkable": The chemical purifier must have been working overtime, sustained, perhaps, by generous pinches of salt! Remember, too. that there was no periscope as such devices had yet to be invented so navigation must have been a problem! Eventually the Resurgam put into Rhyl for repairs.

But, as Frankie Howerd would have said: "Don't mock!" It was, after all, the first of its kind and even if the claims made for it at the time were extravagant, it undoubtedly worked as a submarine.

Improvements and modifications were made and from time to time the boat was taken out on trials. In February 1880 the Resurgam left Rhyl to go to Portsmouth where it was to be evaluated by the Admiralty, but the departure time was in the darkness at 10 pm with a gale warning in force.

The boat was towed by Garrett's steam yacht, "Elfin", but battered by the gale she had trouble with her boilers and as the weather worsened the tow broke, the Resurgam went adrift and eventually sank. The Elfin herself was also lost in the River Dee where she had run for shelter.

So that was the end of the Resurgam and despite many attempts to locate her, she was never found. Over a century later, however, in November 1995, trawlerman Dennis Hunt's trawl hit the Resurgam somewhere between Rhyl and Prestatyn.

The Resurgam was still in one piece, not buried in the sea bed so, without doubt, she will eventually rise again.

On the waves at Rhyl? My brother Brian.

Brian is two and a half years younger than me, born in January 1926. Brian and I both went to Rhyl Convent school and then on to Epworth College, Rhyl. Brian was always keen on the sea and during the summer he loved to help on the pleasure boats that plied from Rhyl beach. To describe Brian as one of the "good guys" of his world is an understatement: He is a good Christian, in the truest sense of the word: Not in any way stuffy or self righteous but always ready to help the elderly or anyone in need. I am very fortunate indeed to have him for a brother.

Brian has an impish sense of humour and was always marvellous with children: Home on leave he would conduct running battles with the neighbourhood children, all armed with water pistols. He would race over the garden walls with the children in full cry on his heels, water pistols blazing away. Mothers would join the fray, hurling buckets of water, though usually with little success! Great fun for all concerned.

Brian was never a motorcyclist: I once forced him to ride my Model X along the lane by Ty Newydd Farm, Rhyl, but it didn't take! Nowadays, however, he is a very keen cyclist, on his bike every evening of the year and in summer time, riding 25/30 miles after dinner.

Brian decided on a life at sea so started on the "Conway" which was one of the last of the Navy's wooden warships before the days of steam. She had survived and was used as a training ship for young Merchant Navy cadets. After their training on the Conway they would join the Merchant Navy as cadet officers.

The Conway was static i.e. she was on permanent moorings and did not go out to sea. Her base was Liverpool but at the outbreak of war she was towed to the Menai Straits. After the War she was being towed back to her berth in Liverpool when the tow line parted and the Conway ran aground immovably in the Menai Straits and it was impossible to re-float her: A sad end for such a unique maritime survival.

After completing his course on the Conway Brian sailed for America on the Q.E.2 on Easter Monday, April 10th 1944. He was to join one of the Liberty ships, the Sam Holt. The Americans had raced ahead in producing these ships in record time, sweeping aside tradition and getting the job done. They were about ten thousand tons and the steel plates were of all welded construction, not riveted. Old sea dogs swore they would fall to pieces in heavy seas, but they didn't!

The Sam Holt joined what was said to be the largest convoy of the War, up to that time, crossing the Atlantic to Loch Ewe on the west coast of Scotland. This huge sea loch was a gathering point for the Atlantic convoys and was protected from submarine attack by boom defences.

From Loch Ewe the Sam Holt was to proceed to London via the North of Scotland and then her task was to transport everything from ammunition to beer to Mulberry Harbour off the Normandy coast, starting a few days after D Day. So Brian was there facing

81

German bombs and bullets as the Sam Holt shuttled to and from England to Mulberry Harbour carrying essential supplies.

Brian served until the end of the War and survived, unlike so many brave men in the Merchant and Royal Navies.

(Top) Rhyl lifeboat, the Caroline Richardson. Man powered like
Ben Hur and in service at Rhyl from 1897 to 1939 when Rhyl
finally changed to a powered lifeboat.
(Left) This is one of the steamers that plied between Rhyl and
Llandudno before World War One. She is loading at the Voryd
pier.

(Top) Perchance to dream, nineteen forties. With motorcycling curtailed during the War, many enthusiasts designed "ideal" machines to be produced after the War. The Beaumont Radial was one of them. The style was certainly futuristic and the three cylinder radial four stroke engine was to be petroil lubricated and turbo *discharged*. Needless to say, none were made.

(Bottom) Perchance to dream, nineteen hundreds. Surely the Evart Hall was never made. Four to fifty mph claimed. Engine started by pushing switch or foot lever. No self starter so presumably by moving the ignition lever to create a spark when the contact points opened and hoping this would turn the engine over. The World War One American "Liberty" engines were coil ignition and could sometimes be started like this.

Chapter Thirteen
Engineering Apprenticeship

My mother, before her marriage, had been the secretary to Herbert Matthews, the Works Manager of George Fletcher and Co., Litchurch Lane, Derby. He was still the Works Manager and I was taken on as a "Privileged Apprentice" to go through the works with a starting salary of ten shillings and sixpence a week (fifty two and a half pence, if you have forgotten!)

So I moved to Derby and into a very different world.

When living in Rhyl you took for granted the advantage of living in a holiday town and Rhyl society, too, was very pleasant indeed: All parents wanted a better world for their children and this meant a good education. Even if there was not a lot of money in the household, middle class values prevailed.

Derby, however, was a real culture shock! A drab industrial town with rows and rows of terraced houses filled with the workers who manned the town's factories. A working class world and although there must have been a middle class society hidden somewhere, I was never fortunate enough to find it! Roy Hattersley has written evocatively of Sheffield in that era and Derby was just the same.

A colleague of my mother's in her days at George Fletcher and Co. was "Kit" Cotterill who lived in Lower Dale Road, Derby, next to the garage run by Kit and her husband, Syd. Their two sons, Maurice and Alan, were also to go into the motor trade. I needed somewhere to live when I moved to Derby and Kit Cotterill had recommended Mrs. Randle of 128 Stonehill Road and that was where I was to stay until I got married, aged 25.

Stonehill Road is a street of terraced houses known as "palisaded villas" in estate agent speak i.e. not directly onto the pavement as in Coronation Street but with a tiny space in front with a low brick wall topped with a barrier of railings, though all were to be taken for scrap during the War.

Mrs. Randle was a kindly person, as was her husband Joe, but it was, of course, an entirely different society from the one I had known in Rhyl.

George Fletcher's was a large engineering works housed in huge corrugated iron buildings. I could be mistaken but I cannot remember any kind of heating but even if there was it must have been very rudimentary and you had to work to keep warm! Huge overhead cranes ran the length of the fitting and boiler shops and the floors, other than in the machine shops, were earth. Not nice, solid hard packed earth but loose red earth that penetrated socks and anything else it could think of! The whole place totally drab consisting of depressing greys and dreary browns.

In addition to this drab picture the predominant impression was noise.. ear splitting noise. ....Lathes were driven by clattering belts from overhead lineshafting and every kind of machine competed to make even more noise than its neighbour: Rattles, clanks, thumps, bangs. Every possible combination and cacophony of sound. Am I describing Dante's Inferno? Not really, but there could have been a family resemblance!

All very different from strolling along Rhyl promenade!

We started work at 7.55 am and finished at 5.30 pm. with an hour's break for lunch, sorry, dinner. Long hours and hard going for a youngster from Rhyl.

George Fletcher and Co. were established in the 1860's to make sugar manufacturing machinery. In those days sugar was produced from sugar cane in the West Indies: The cane was crushed by huge cast iron rollers, like a gigantic mangle and the juice was processed to make sugar. Fletcher's made everything required for sugar manufacture and equipped complete factories.

Later on, sugar was also made from sugar beet in Europe and the process, other than crushing the cane, was much the same.

During the War the factory was largely turned over to War production though as dollars were desperately needed to pay for

Chapter Fourteen
Light in the Gloom

So a drab industrial town. Work in a drab, noisy colourless factory. The war news almost unfailingly grim. So was there anything to lighten the gloom? Of course there was! First of all we were young with the irrepressible high spirits and optimism of youth and, despite everything, there were still opportunities to relax and enjoy ourselves

Firstly, of course, was the cinema. The cinemas were huge, luxurious palaces of entertainment and "Going to the flicks" was an essential part of the week's entertainment. The cinemas were packed, too, with queues to get in at weekends. We enjoyed the films of the period immensely, and what classics some of them were; they have certainly stood the test of time.

In 1996 I had to travel through North Manchester and what a sight it was: The whole area a devastated wasteland, an ideal situation for a film producer looking for a location to film the Somme, 1916! Whole areas of terraced housing demolished but every few hundred yards a cinema still stood intact, its Art Deco architecture crumbling and blackened: Melancholy monuments to the days when they were unchallenged palaces of entertainment. Most were empty, derelict, but a few amazingly still attempted to struggle on with "Bingo" scrawled in huge white letters on their frontages, no doubt awaiting the arrival of the bulldozer for their final coup de grace.

But in the 1940's, all that was in the future and the cinemas reigned supreme.

Another important entertainment for young people were the dance halls with the marvellous music of that era. I resolved to learn to dance and attended The London School of Dancing, Babington Lane, Derby run by Mr. and Mrs. Talbot. We danced to the records of Victor Sylvester and his "Strict tempo" music for dancing.

This was a chance to meet other young people and dance with the pretty girls of my age group. Few of us at that age had regular girlfriends and certainly not me! I thoroughly enjoyed taking girls to dances and enjoyed a light-hearted relationship with a chaste goodnight kiss, but that was all.

One of the girls I danced with regularly at the London School was Margaret Swan. She used to attend with her sister, Joan, two lovely girls. Margaret and I danced well together and I remember Mr. Talbot instructing Margaret and I in the Tango; "In the Tango there is no rise, no fall, no sway!"

Margaret also worked at Fletcher's, as a tracer: In those days the engineering drawings had to be traced in ink on a kind of opaque cloth from which blueprints or their successor, whiteprints, were taken.

Learning to dance was very much the right thing to do and gave me many hours of enjoyment. Margaret and Joan had a brother Bob who was in the Navy and they both hero worshipped him. Bob was to survive the war, despite being on the Dorsetshire when she was sunk by the Japanese, and marry another lovely, vivacious girl who was in the WRNS. Her name was Elizabeth Griffiths who lived in Stone and I was to meet her later. We have stayed in touch ever since though, strangely enough, I was not to meet Bob until after the War.

Petrol was still available, though rationed, so I was able to enjoy motorcycling with new countryside to explore and, most important, I began to buy and sell motorcycles. Yes that was still possible, even in wartime, so that became an enjoyable and profitable hobby.

Once I got used to working in Dante's Inferno, sorry, Fletcher's, things weren't so bad after all! I was, of course, immensely keen to learn all I could about engineering and the use of tools so there was a lot to learn and Ernie was a willing and competent tutor. I was, in fact, to stay with him until I eventually moved into the Machine Shops. Ernie and I became great friends and I also got to know a wide circle of workmates at Fletcher's together with fellow students at Derby Technical College. I was allowed one day a week at Technical College which was a marvellous break, but the evening classes after a hard day's work were not so good!

Engineering minded young men took to motorcycles like ducks to water so I soon met a wide range of motorcycle enthusiasts. I got on well with my workmates at Fletcher's and they were, in the main, a very pleasant company: A few, of course, could well have been described as "remarkable" but they were in the minority!

None of the workers at Fletcher's went to work in a car other than Murray, the Managing director, who lived at Repton. The Works secretary also went to work in a car, a Singer soft top sports car, but that was the lot!

Motorcycles were used some of the time, as petrol allowed, and there were some interesting machines: Freddie Phillpot from the Boiler Shop had a 1938 250cc Rudge Rapid in immaculate order. On leaving work it always started first kick with a burst of throttle.

There were two chaps from the West Indies who were "Privileged apprentices" like me. One was named Hutson, something of an oddball; pleasant enough, but not very communicative! Older than me, he eventually married a Derby girl, The other was named Charlie but whose surname I have forgotten. He had a 1938 350cc Levis, twin port, upswept pipes. Again in excellent order and how we envied him this lovely machine. He also had a 1930 500cc ohv Ariel, just for fun, with valve gear that sounded like a football rattle. I eventually bought it from him for ten bob.

An old-timer named Bill worked in the Grinding Shop in charge of two huge grinding wheels. He was of 5x5 configuration and came from Sheffield with that harsh Sheffield accent and quaint Yorkshire phrases that were new to me. Sentences would be ended with "Tha' knows", a marvellous all purpose phrase with multiple meanings: It could mean "as you well know", "as you might know" or "as you certainly should know" and numerous other variations. Another Yorkshire phrase new to me was "Mekkit a bit summat like" which meant "When you have completed that job, please ensure that it is finished to an acceptable standard".

Yorkshire is, as far as I know, the only county that takes a pride in its skinflint status: "If ever tha' does owt for nowt, see tha' does it for thissen." A phrase with the dual purpose of demonstrating the

Yorkshire philosophy and accent. Not, I hasten to add, that this motto ever applied to Bill who had a most generous nature, but I do know a Yorkshireman....

Most other counties do not pride themselves on their parsimony but on their stupidity, claiming as their own the following couplet:

"Derbyshire born, Derbyshire bred,
Strong in the arm and weak in the head"

For Derbyshire, of course, you can substitute any other county. The problem is that they have mixed up the true meaning! The original wording was "wick" in the head which meant sharp. Just thought you'd like to know!

Bill had a 1929 250cc side-valve Matchless, laid up during the war and was very proud of a go-faster accessory he had fitted : A "Spoorts Exost". By this he meant a megaphone silencer! A keen fisherman he used to ride the seven miles from Shardlow to Derby in seven minutes but the little Matchless, with or without its spoorts exost, would be hard pressed to struggle up to a maximum speed of 50mph, so how did he do it?

At Alvaston as you leave Derby there was a row of shops and above one of them was a large clock. As Bill hurtled by he would look at the time and on reaching Shardlow would look at the church clock seven minutes later. In Bill's eyes this meant an average speed of sixty miles an hour! The seven miles, in reality, was from Derby town centre to Shardlow and the clock at Alvaston was almost half way to Shardlow, but I never had the heart to disillusion him!

On autumn Sunday mornings Bill and I would often head for Shardlow on our push bikes to fish in the canal, usually returning with a good catch. Mrs. Randle would kindly cook my share for me and I would steel myself to eat them: I must say, however, that even when heavily salted they bore no comparison to sea fish.

Derby did not suffer from bombing as much as some other Midlands towns but it certainly did not escape. The wail of the air raid sirens would send everyone down into their air raid shelters. Many homes had Anderson Shelters in the garden: These were made of corrugated iron and dug into the ground with a layer of earth on top. You slept on bunk beds and as there was no heating it was bitterly cold. I eventually gave up and stayed in bed!

So the German bombers were often overhead and the menacing, strangely uneven note of their engines became a familiar sound. Bombs never hit Stonehill Road but they did fall nearby when Derby was the target and you would cycle to work next morning dodging bomb craters in the road and with the fronts of houses blown out.

To deter the bombers, barrage balloons were tethered at every available spot, the sites manned by W.A.A.F.'s. In addition to that a smokescreen enveloped the town during the night. This was done by having a series of peculiar contraptions comprising a circular base and a chimney, all made in galvanised sheet metal. The base was filled with a mixture of paraffin and old sump oil. The Pioneer Corps were in charge and when the devices were ignited huge clouds of evil smelling smoke billowed out. There were rows of them in Stonehill Road and neighbouring streets so it was impossible to completely keep out the fumes. Was this smoke screen effective? Hard to tell, but it must have made important targets like the Rolls Royce factories a more difficult target for the German bombers.

One night in eight was spent "Firewatching" in the factory in which you worked, ready to put out any fires started by the bombing. My friend T and I, however, soon joined the 102 Battalion Home Guard to man anti-aircraft rocket launchers. About forty of them were located in Mickleover, Derby, to launch 40 rockets in unison at German bombers.

It is almost impossible to grasp the magnitude of the U Boat losses and, of course, the scale of these losses was not made public at the time. In 1940 almost one and a half million tons of allied shipping was lost. In 1941, two and a half million tons and in 1942 an incredible five and a half million tons.

To the German U-boat Grey Wolf packs this was their "Happy Time" and if losses had continued at this rate the War would have been won for Germany. Finally, however, the tide was turned and the most important factor was the breaking of the German code enabling the Allies to know the routes the U-boats were taking.

Not only were we dependent on food, munitions and raw materials from America but all petrol came from America, too, so that vital lifeline across the Atlantic was essential to our survival.

With their engineering background there was no shortage of motorcycle enthusiasts at Fletcher's. A big man in the Pattern Shop had a 1934 350cc Overhead Camshaft Velocette but laid up for the War: It was his intention to send it back to the factory after the War for rebuilding but, of course, such facilities were never to be available again.

These overhead camshaft Velocettes, or "Camshaft Vellers" as they were known in Derby, were beautifully made machines, highly regarded by engineering minded young men. Velocettes had won the T.T. with one in 1926 and had gone on to battle with Nortons in the T.T.'s of the 1930's.

Another man had a beautifully kept 350 A.J.S of the late thirties and a cheery little machinist had a nineteen thirty five *and a half* 350! An older fitter named Hepton, a man of incredible parsimony, had a 1936 500 ohv Sunbeam with four-speed, hand-change gearbox but, once again, laid up for the War. Come to think of it, he was a Yorkshireman!

A chap who worked at Derby Carriage-side, where they made railway rolling stock, had a mid 1930's 150cc Federation made by the Co-op! Twin port with an incredibly noisy exhaust but the only one I ever remember seeing on the road.

Apprentices like me had a selection of older bikes, often in the process of restoration or "Doing up" as the phrase was in those days. As I had quickly started to buy and sell motorcycles I rented a garage at the bottom of Stonehill Road and bikes were stored and repaired there: As I got more and more involved there would be seven or eight bikes for sale.

My starting wage at Fletcher's was ten shillings and sixpence a week (fifty two and a half pence). Digs were thirty five shillings and, in addition, I had to be clothed, maintained and have some spending money: All provided by my mother. Bikes would be sold with a profit margin of five to ten pounds which was a lot of money compared to my weekly wage.

A bike bought for £25 would be sold for about £30. One bought for £60, sold for £70. But in those days prices were considerably lower for earlier machines.

An older man named George worked in the Pattern Shop. He lived near West Hallam and had supplementary petrol to come to and from work. His bike was a 1932 500 side-valve Raleigh and sidecar, a very well used machine with cylinder bore so worn that it had virtually no compression. Even so, however, it ran reliably and at a later date I bought it from him for seven pounds ten shillings. I rode it to Rhyl one summer holiday with my pal George Peet in the sidecar. Flat out speed downhill was 45mph! I later sold it for twelve pounds ten shillings!

On one occasion when riding the Raleigh combination I ran out of petrol at Spondon. No petrol coupons so I put half a gallon of paraffin in the petrol tank. The engine was still hot and I managed to push start the outfit. It got me home, somehow, belching out black paraffin fumes and struggling up to about 25mph flat out!

Another motorcycle enthusiast I met at the time was Jack Gibson. He had owned a number of International Nortons in the thirties but did not have a machine of his own then. He worked with his parents at a grocery shop in Cheapside, Derby, opposite John Wallace, Ironmonger. Wallaces were in business when my mother was a girl.

Jack was a born mechanic and had a lock up garage nearby, off Curzon Street. He had a part time business repairing cars and motorcycles and I often used to help him at weekends. Jack was an instinctive engineer and should have gone into the motor trade after the War but he failed to do so and stayed in the grocery shop which, of course, eventually had to close as the grocery trade changed.

There was a lot to be learned from Jack and the machines he repaired. He made an excellent job of restoring a 150 ohv B.S.A. for the wife of a surgeon at the Derbyshire Royal Infirmary. It was fitted with a Maglita (Pronounced mag-lighter). They were diabolical instruments that purported to provide a spark to run the engine and a current to charge the battery from the same instrument. A magdyno, of course, was entirely different: It had a magneto for ignition and sitting neatly on top was an independent dynamo.

Magdynos worked very well indeed: Maglitas didn't! They were, in fact, trouble whenever I encountered them: They struggled to emit a dreary spark and, if you were very lucky, about one and a half amps oozed out in a half hearted attempt to charge the battery!

Jack had replaced the Maglita on the B.S.A. with a Magdyno which on this particular machine then ran at engine speed, giving an "idle" spark, i.e. there was a spark every time the piston reached the top of its stroke: Even so, it worked perfectly well.

Jack had a customer named Jagger who owned a 1935 Triumph Gloria open sports car. A lovely car I thought then, and still do. He had a very well kept 150 Coventry Eagle, late nineteen thirties, which he wanted to sell for £15. I offered to sell it for him and sold it for £25, splitting the £10 profit with my pal, Harry Tunaley, "T".

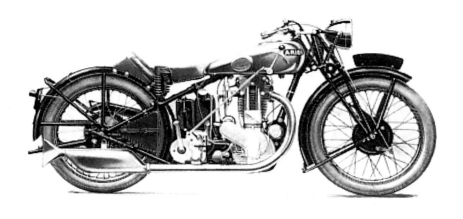

(Top) 1930 500cc ohv Ariel. I bought one from fellow apprentice Charlie for ten bob! It ran perfectly well despite valve gear that sounded like a football rattle!
(Left) Sidevalve Matchless about 1930. This is the big brother of Bill's two fifty.

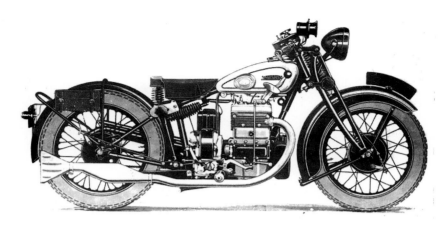

(Top) 1930 400cc Matchless Silver Arrow, twin cylinder, spring frame. Full marks for adventurous design but never destined to be a sales success. It looks like a vertical twin with its compact, one piece cylinder block but it was, in fact, a narrow angle vee twin. The sidevalve engine relegated it to the role of gentle tourer, which limited its appeal.

(Bottom) 1929 sidevalve Norton. This is the 633cc "Big Four". Why "Big Four" when it was neither four cylinder or four valve? Don't know! The reason is lost in antiquity! It was, however, the big brother of the 500cc 16H, the machine that gave the Tunaley brothers their introduction to motorcycling.

Chapter Fifteen
I meet Harry Tunaley

I first met Harry Tunaley, always known as "T", at Derby Technical College and I already knew his older brother, Arnold.

T was one of the "good guys" of this world: A very pleasant young man of enormous integrity. We established an immediate "rapport" and became firm friends. We had, of course, a shared interest in motorcycles and worked away together during every spare moment at the single car asbestos garage I rented at the bottom of Stonehill Road. He was another instinctive "hands on" engineer combined with an additional flair for auto-electrics.

T had a marvellous sense of humour and a happy turn of phrase: For example L Plates were "Destination Plates" and "A fish on his face" was like "A chip on his shoulder", only worse! T maintained that to take your driving test in London they sent you round the block and if you came back without blood on the front bumper, you'd passed! Someone who couldn't keep a secret was a "blob-gob". T's wit and intelligence ensured that he sparkled in any company.

T and his brother Arnold had bought, for a few shillings, an ancient French "Clip-on" engine to fit on a bicycle. These engines were made in France in the 1920's and although not a success then, the idea was to continue and be used successfully years later by, for example, Velo Solex.

The engine was fitted over the front wheel of an ordinary bicycle and you pushed down a lever to press the drive roller onto the front tyre, lifting the lever to disengage the drive.

T and his brother did manage to persuade the venerable engine to splutter into life but it never ran properly and was clearly never destined to get them on the road.

I, however, had the answer to their problem: A 1930 500cc side-valve model 16H Norton, price £2. The piston had blown its top off but a second hand replacement could be found for a few shillings.

The insurmountable barrier was that £2 as their entire capital, all thirty shillings of it, was tied up in that confounded clip on.

So I had an idea: Without telling them I put an advert. in the "Derby Evening Telegraph" under their address offering the engine for sale at £2.

To their amazement a customer turned up and bought it for the £2 asked so with their capital restored, plus an extra ten bob, they were able to buy the Norton. They quickly found and fitted a replacement piston and got the Norton back on the road and, as far as I remember, it gave them good service and was their first motorcycle.

I had originally bought the Norton for £5 and had ridden it to Rhyl but on the return journey, halfway between Nantwich and Stone, there was a loud bang and the top blew off the piston.

I pushed the bike to the nearest station, Pipegate, consigned it to be returned by goods train and I returned to Derby by passenger train.

Later on when their finances were in better shape they did graduate to better machines. T bought a 1930 400cc Matchless "Silver Arrow" which was a very advanced design in its day. Most machines of that era were single cylinder, rigid frame but the Silver Arrow was a narrow angle vee twin with the cylinders in line with the frame and so close together that they were contained in a single cylinder block, a very compact arrangement. It also had swinging arm rear suspension, like machines of today.

The sidevalve engine meant that performance was never sparkling as they were designed as refined tourers and, strangely enough, motorcycles of unusual capacities i.e. neither 250, 350 or 500cc never seem to sell very well, so despite its advanced design the Silver Arrow never broke sales records.

A year later Matchless produced an even more revolutionary machine, the 1,000cc four cylinder vee-twin, overhead camshaft

Silver Hawk, again with swinging arm rear suspension. Sales, however, were even worse than those of the Silver Arrow and I never saw one on the road.

At the same time that Matchless produced the Silver Hawk, Ariel introduced their Square Four, a design that was to be a great success and would continue in updated form into the post-war era.

T finally bought a very well kept original 1936 350 ohv Ariel for £25 from a man in St. Albans Road, Derby.

Arnold never lost his interest in motorcycles despite a spell on old and exasperatingly unreliable machines. On a later occasion, when he was living in the Nottingham area, T received a letter from him with a sketch map showing the location of a 150cc ohv New Imperial. It had broken down for the umpteenth time so Arnold had shoved it behind a hedge and abandoned it: If T would care to collect it he could have it!

T and I did collect it, got it going perfectly well, and gave it back to Arnold, reasoning that his hasty decision to give it away would be regretted! Arnold also progressed to better and better machines and on the way bought a 1930 ohv B.S.A. Sloper of about 1930 vintage. We thought it looked very old fashioned but were amazed by the impressive surge of power when you opened the throttle. He finally bought a very well kept 500 Ariel of the late thirties.

Arnold now lives in America and finally ended up with B.M.W. twins. In 1984 he changed to a B.M.W. 1,000cc four cylinder in which he has travelled over 180,000 miles, During the early 1990's, with his wife in the sidecar, they embarked on an ambitious tour of America, lasting several months. They repeated this in 1998 with another marathon ten thousand mile journey. "Once a motorcyclist, always a motorcyclist" is perfectly true in Arnold's case.

Christmas 1940 was my first opportunity for a break from Fletcher's. I had a week's holiday and badly needed it! Off I went on my Triumph for a winter journey to Rhyl and to a different world. Stella Maris was, of course, still filled with the lovely girls I knew so it was a marvellous homecoming.

Christmas at Stella Maris was always magical and never more so then in those days: The whole place would be swinging and in the evenings we would clear the dining room for dances with our radiogram to provide the music. Everyone had a marvellous time.

Dances in the town, too and at Stella Maris charades and party games galore: the whole of the Christmas period was a hectic and joyous time for everyone. We enjoyed every minute and danced far into the night. Light-hearted kisses, too? Of course, lots of them!

A sad day, then, when it was time to climb onto my Triumph and head back to Derby and the drab, noisy world of Fletcher's!

Another bright spot was reading "The Motor Cycle" (the Blue 'un) and "Motorcycling" (the Green 'un). They kept us in touch with the world of motorcycling even after the basic petrol ration was eventually withdrawn. There were informative articles of all kinds, road tests of bikes of the thirties and articles about machines of the past.

Graham Walker, editor of Motorcycling, was an ex T.T. rider who had ridden from 1920 to 1934. He had been in the lead in the 1929 T.T. on his Rudge when the engine seized due to the oil supply having been cut back too drastically. He won the Lightweight T.T. in 1931 on a Rudge and in his last year, 1934 was third in the Lightweight Class on a 250 Rudge and sixth in the Senior on a 500 Rudge. What marvellous bikes those racing Rudges of that era were.

Graham Walker wrote a series of articles entitled "Seen From the Saddle", starting with his first T.T. and continuing to his last year. They were superbly written, giving the prospects and hopes before the race and an account of the races themselves, literally seen from the saddle.

His son, Murray Walker, went on to become the universally admired Grand Prix commentator of today and he, too, remained a motorcycle enthusiast having only recently given up riding B.M.W.'s.

J.J. Hall was an ex Brooklands rider, then a captain in the army training dispatch riders. He wrote a series of articles about vintage motorcycles, sparking off an interest in them that has never waned.

Vintage bikes were unearthed from all over the place and went to enthusiasts to restore. This was, without doubt, the start of the vintage motorcycle movement. Reading about the machines of the past gave me an interest in vintage motorcycles and the evolution of the internal combustion engine that has been a lifelong pleasure.

Older enthusiasts at Fletcher's, too, drew on their memories so there was lots to learn and the bikes I was buying and selling were, of course, already part of motorcycling history.

All sorts of bikes were bought and sold: Rudges, Nortons, B.S.A.'s. of all kinds, Royal Enfields, Velocettes, A.J.S.'s, Matchless and many more. Among odd makes bought I remember a 1927 250 Rex Acme with a Blackburne engine, a 1927 vee-twin 680 New Imperial that was entirely covered with a light surface of rust. It started and ran well though sounded like a circular saw!.

We painted the whole thing black over the rust and advertised it. Customers complained that it should not have been painted over like that but the answer was that they would not have bought it if they had seen it as it was originally! It was finally sold for £12.10s.

I was also quite involved with 250cc overhead camshaft Excelsior Manxmen and if ever a motorcycle looked right it was the Manxman. They looked as if they were straining to leap away even when standing still. I bought and sold quite a few and ex T.T. winner, H.G, Tyrell Smith who had raced them in the 1930's was very helpful in supplying spares. You would need a lot of money to buy one now.

Another bike I remember well was a 1925 770cc B.S.A vee twin complete with sidecar: Complete and running it sold for £15.

Rudges, too were frequently bought and sold and we got to know them well. We liked the 1931 and onwards models with rearward facing magnetos as we considered the earlier ones with forward facing magnetos old fashioned! They had lots of power, handled very well indeed and we got to know them inside and out.

Another privileged apprentice was a handsome young man with a zany sense of humour named Peter Stewart, inevitably known as "Stew". Stew had the benefit of a good education and lived with his uncle and aunt in Derby: His uncle was Fletcher's Representative. Stew had a 1930 Montgomery, powered by a

500cc ohv J.A.P. engine. He carefully restored the machine and made a very good job of it: It would be a very rare machine today.

But Harold Kerry stands out as a truly dedicated enthusiast: First of all he was a Scott enthusiast and to understand Scotts and persuade them to give of their best you had to have a special flair. Set the oil supply for high speed and they would oil plugs at modest speeds. Set for modest speeds and they would be starved of oil at high speeds: So how did you get it right? By flair and that very special mechanical feel that Scotts demanded of their owners.

Harold and I decided to construct an electrically powered motorcycle which could, of course, be ridden without restriction as no petrol was required. The favoured power unit was a "Dynamotor" from a Bullnose Morris. This was a dual purpose instrument: Press the starter button on a Bullnose and the Dynamotor acted as a self starter. As the speed built up it served as the dynamo.

As it was such a heavy duty instrument the bearings were of generous proportions so it was ideal for our purpose. We took the 98cc Villiers engine out of an Excelsior and replaced it with the Dynamotor. A large twelve volt battery mounted across the frame and we were ready to go.

Harold lived at Stanley Common near Derby so the bike was wheeled out onto the road and I climbed aboard and pressed the starter button. This simple system gave full power immediately so the bike leapt forward to achieve its maximum speed of about 10mph! We had retained the original two speed gearbox so we were far too low geared but it was great for the village children who ran alongside, cheering!

Had we spent more time on development, getting the gearing right and arranging a system of resistances so that you started out on low power, the bike would have been perfectly practical, but we did not continue with the experiment.

Alf Briggs, however, the Derby racing motorcyclist, did construct a battery powered motorcycle during those years which he used successfully to keep him on the road.

Harold had hopes of road racing after the War and bought a 1936 500cc Manx Norton. As far as I know, however, it was never

Chapter Sixteen
An Epic Ride

A bike I have good reason to remember was a 1934 600cc Panther. These 600cc Panthers were really intended for sidecar haulage but I rode this one solo. It had a powerful slow revving engine and the sloping engine took the place of the front downtube.

Handling for this particular bike was peculiar: It had a constant steering wobble but a firm grip made it worse! You just had to rest your hands lightly on the handlebars and get used to it!

One winter's night I set off for Rhyl after work and was happily bowling along the Uttoxeter Road at about 45mph when I saw a red light at the side of the road which I took to be a warning of road works. Keeping to the centre of the road I kept going without slackening speed.

A moment later I hit a solid wall of water which completely winded me and blotted out all vision: I could neither breathe or see!

The red light had been a warning of flood water and I had ploughed right into it.

The bike stopped, of course, and I was soaked to the skin though, surprisingly, I had managed to stay on it. The sensible thing to do would have been to turn round and go back to Derby, about ten miles away but, no, I started the bike up again and went on.

Progressing slowly in bottom gear I got through the flood water without further trouble and used the same method for getting through further stretches of flood water up to Uttoxeter.

Uttoxeter to Stone is hilly so not too bad until I got to Field: Quite deep flood water there but, once again, I got through.

Stone to Nantwich brought further stretches, all negotiated successfully and about five miles before Nantwich I stopped at an army camp to get warm for a short while in front of the coke stove in the gatehouse.

More floodwater at times and when I got to Nantwich there was flood water over the road roaring over the river bridge. A sign said *"dangerous, do not cross"* but I took a chance and went over anyway! Over half a century later the bridge is still standing!

On again through Tarporley and Chester, meeting stretches of flood water but never too bad. From Chester onwards onto the top road so no flood water and all was well.

Down at last into the Vale of Clwyd where I usually turned right below Rhuallt onto the Rhuddlan Road. The road, however was barred off with a notice *"Closed due to flood water"*. Nothing for it, then, but to go on via St. Asaph.

Once onto the dual carriageway out of St. Asaph I encountered long stretches of flood water so I kept to the centre of the road where the water was shallowest. Finally I hit a bad patch which got deeper and deeper until it became impossible to continue but I had a brilliant idea!....Ride on the centre reservation!

Great! On I went but soon even the centre reservation was covered with water and it was like riding across the surface of a huge lake with water stretching as far as I could see on either side: A unique motorcycling experience!

Even so, I kept going until suddenly I found myself hurtling through the air over the handlebars: Every now and then they put little tombstones to indicate a water hydrant below and my front wheel had hit one which was, of course, submerged!

I was wet through anyway, couldn't get any wetter, so I hauled the Panther upright out of the water and, amazingly, it started up again. I finally got to the point when the water was swirling past my feet and although they were on the footrests they were submerged! How the magneto kept sparking I'll never know!

At last I approached the bridge just before Rhuddlan: Reach the bridge and I would be clear. At that point, however, the rivers Elwy and Clwyd converge so the combined floodwaters were raging across the road.

Surely it was quite impossible to go further: The dual carriageway ended and the short stretch of road to the bridge was even lower. On the left hand side of the road was a hedge and, no doubt, a grass verge which was submerged and the water was cascading through the hedge at a tremendous rate.

I put the bike on its stand on the last part of the submerged dual carriageway and waded through the water to the submerged grass verge. The water tore past my legs and was the deepest I had yet encountered but the grass verge was higher than the roadway though the current was strongest. Could the bike get through? Only thing to do was to try it!

Kicked the bike into life again and headed it into the flood water, somehow managing to reach the grass verge. Once onto the grass verge the flood water tore at the bike, pushing it sideways. The bike slid and bounced. Feet well under water now as the bike slithered and bucked: Surely the Mag MUST be well under water now and the engine MUST stop! But, no, it kept going somehow and I emerged safely onto the bridge and home at last!.

Those visits to Rhyl were the highlights that kept me going during those drab years. Rhyl was a different world and a marvellous break so I went over at every possible opportunity. I was often accompanied by my friends and my mother always made us all welcome and found us accommodation, always "on the house".

Running Stella Maris during those war years must have been a tremendous headache with blackout, rationing and shortages of every kind, not to mention the problem of staff.

Released from Fletcher's for the Easter holiday 1941 I rode over to Rhyl on my newly acquired 250 Panther. Now these machines were built down to a price but, even so, were an excellent design. By 1939 all sales of the basic model were handled by the big London Dealers, Pride and Clarke and sold for the incredibly low price of £29.17.6. This figure is as indelibly stamped on the memory of every 1930's motorcyclist as 1066 is stamped on every schoolboy's!

My 1934 model was three speed hand change and had been carefully maintained. It ran very well with a healthy exhaust note and I was delighted with it on the run over.

Halfway to Rhyl I saw a motorcycle broken down at the roadside with the rider and pillion passenger trying to get it started. The bike was a 1930 James with a 250cc Villiers two-stroke engine. The rider was "Chesh" Cheshire and his pillion passenger Philip Griffiths, both from Stone, Staffordshire.

Between us we managed to locate the trouble and soon had the machine running again. I then asked where they were going and was surprised to hear that their destination was Rhyl, for the Easter holiday. "Where are you staying?" I asked, only to be told that they had nothing arranged but were going "on spec." "Right" I said "It will have to be Stella Maris". On we went for a trouble free run to Rhyl and my mother found my new found friends accommodation at very modest cost.

We got together, of course, and toured the Vale of Clwyd with Philip riding pillion on the James. I had the superior machine, overhead valve compared to Chesh's humble two-stroke. Inevitably we had to compete to see who had the faster machine and to my great embarrassment the James beat the Panther every time! We all thoroughly enjoyed that holiday and they were, of course, absolutely delighted to be introduced to the lovely girls staying at Stella Maris.

On the way back to Derby I called in at Philip's home and was made most welcome by his mother and family. She was a widow and ran a hairdressing business in the big three story house going out of Stone on the right hand side.

They were a lively, cheery family and Philip had an attractive and vivacious younger sister named Elizabeth. Elizabeth was to eventually join the WRNS, meet Bob Swan from Derby and marry him! Bob, of course, was the brother of Margaret and Joan whom I had met at the London School of Dancing. From then on I would often call in on my way back from Rhyl and despite, on occasion, being soaking wet I was always made welcome.

I went over to stay with Chesh and his family one weekend and met his father who had worked as a tester for Triumph in Coventry both before and after World War One. He had also raced Triumphs in the early days so he was a most interesting chap with many stories of those days.

After the war Triumphs had introduced their new "Baby" model with 225cc two-stroke engine and two-speed gearbox when most machines were still single-gear and belt-drive. A customer brought one back to the factory complaining of excessive vibration: Cheshire took it out on test but could find nothing wrong. Reporting to the customer he explained that other than some vibration when flat out in bottom gear there was nothing wrong with the machine. "What do you mean, bottom gear?" said the customer!

On one occasion T and I rode to Rhyl together: I rode the 600 Panther and he rode a 1932 500 ohv Levis. Now the Levis was in many ways quite an advanced machine, looking more like a late thirties model. It was raining hard on the way over and T, who was a perfectly competent rider, went slower and slower on the bends. Impatiently I waved him down and asked him what was the matter. He complained that in the wet the bike was unpredictable on the bends. Confident that I could handle the beast I changed places

I headed into the first bend without slackening speed only to find that the bike tried to do the splits! In the dry it handled perfectly well but in the wet you just didn't know what the bike was going to do: Once again, they don't make 'em.......

One of the experiences we used to enjoy was taking our bikes down to the beach at Kinmel Bay at night and practice broadsliding on the hard sand just after the tide had gone out. A perfect place to practice the exhilarating technique. The 500 Levis slid beautifully and even a machine as unlikely as the 600 Panther could be persuaded to slide.

On another occasion I rode a 250 Levis to Rhyl, a 1938 model. This performed and handled beautifully with none of the vices of that 1932 500.

I kept the Triumph Model X long after it had been replaced by bigger and more efficient machines but eventually the time came when it had to go. A young chap who lived nearby agreed to buy it at £5 but could he have it first and pay me in two weeks time? Foolishly I agreed.

A month later after he had been riding the machine constantly I asked him for payment. He told me his mother wanted to see me! When I got to the house she asked me how much the machine was when new (£23.17.6) and how old it was. She then got out a pen and paper and with a depreciation factor of her own worked out that the bike must now be worth about tuppence halfpenny! Pointless to explain that with the war and inflation in between you just could not calculate motorcycle values like that though I did say that the agreed price was £5.

The fact that the price had been agreed and so was not negotiable meant nothing to her so I simply took the knocked about Triumph back. Not possible to knock an elderly motorcycle about in a month? Don't you believe it! But she taught both her son and I a lesson: For me, don't let an article go until it is paid for and for her son that his word was worthless. I reckon that my lesson was the more valuable!

My first real motorcycle, bought to keep, not resell, was a 1934 350 overhead camshaft Velocette. As previously mentioned these were beautifully made machines and a joy to ride and handle. I covered many miles on it and it often did the Rhyl run. I was to become a lot more involved with "Camshaft Vellers".

The War had been going for some years when Zec's cartoon appeared in the "Daily Mirror" in March 1942: It showed a blazing oil tanker sinking as the result of enemy action. In the foreground a solitary survivor on a liferaft and the caption was: "The price of petrol has been increased by one penny".

That was the signal for the end of petrol for private motoring or motorcycling. The Basic petrol ration for cars ended at the end of June 1942 but because of the more efficient use of petrol, the motorcycle basic ration continued until the end of October. So what did we do then? Prepare for the return of petrol after the war.

We had decided to try our luck at grasstrack racing so a suitable machine had to be bought, tuned and prepared. The obvious choice, of course, was a "Camshaft Veller". So a suitable machine acquired and work started. In addition, with an eye to post war trials riding I had bought a 1938 350 Tiger 80 Triumph.

What marvellous little machines those Triumphs were; After the War I was to ride mine to and from Rhyl most weekends, ride it for miles over the Clwydian Range, ride it in Trials, Scrambles and even Grasstracks. Snappy performers with excellent handling.

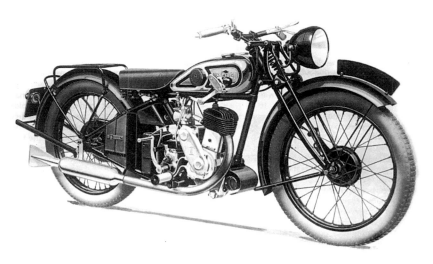

(Top) Panther 600, early 1930's. The cylinder barrel and head of the 500 and 600 Panthers took the place of the front downtube. They were largely regarded as sidecar machines, rather than solo mounts. Strongly made machines capable of endless hard work. (Bottom) Raleigh were one of the great names in motorcycles but due to the recession, production ceased at the end of 1933. This is a 1932 300cc side-valve model, very similar to the 1932 500cc side-valve with sidecar that I owned.

(Top) Goldsworthy Gurney steam coach with which Sir Charles Dance ran regular passenger services between Gloucester and Cheltenham in 1831. Note the steersman at the front.
(Bottom) Hancocks steam coaches that ran regular passenger services in London during the 1830's.

Chapter Seventeen
The Long, Long Trail

When I started motorcycling in 1939 it was very much a motoring age and it felt as if motorcars had been there for ever but, of course, this was far from the case. At that time people in their late forties could remember the time when there were no cars or motorcycles on the road. I have always found the development and evolution of road transport to be of compelling interest and I outline it very briefly here.

It is not generally realised today that between the years 1820 and 1840 there were dozens of steam-powered passenger services operating throughout the country.

Starting in this period Walter Hancock of Stratford operated a series of steam driven regular services in London for about 15 years. From Paddington to the Bank his "Autopsy" and "Era" are reputed to have carried four thousand passengers through a period of nine months at an average speed of 12mph. His last vehicle, the "Automaton" was technically very advanced and was a 22 seater capable of 20mph.

Scott Russell operated no less than six steam coaches between Paisley and Glasgow in 1834 though after a boiler burst, due to a collapsed wheel, five people were killed and the service was stopped by the Court of Sessions. He was, however, later to run steam coach services in London.

Sir Goldsworthy Gurney built a number of successful steam road vehicles with an improved boiler of his own design and these vehicles were used in several parts of the country. Sir Charles Dance, using Gurney vehicles, introduced a four times daily service between Gloucester and Cheltenham.

A Gurney vehicle was used to demonstrate to the War Office its suitability to replace horse drawn coaches and it was reputed to have made the return journey from London to Bath at an average speed of 15mph. Needless to say, it didn't get the job!

There were many other makers, including Redmund, the Heaton brothers, Ogle and Simms, Maudslay etc. and as the 1830's advanced the design of steam coaches leapt ahead: Steam separators, countershafts, differential gears, Ackermann steering, forced draught were all in use yet by 1840 the steam coach era had all but ended.

"Ah", I hear you shout "The Red Flag Act". But this was not the case as the Red Flag Act was not introduced until 1861. It was, indeed, the final death knell for powered road transport when they were restricted to 4mph in the country and 2mph in town. In addition they had to have a footman walking 100 yards ahead with a red flag.

But this was all in the future and before then the speed limit was not too onerous at 5mph in town and 10mph in the country and there was no requirement for a footman ahead with, or without, a red flag.

No, it was not the Government who killed off the early steamers but a number of other factors. Not least important was the enmity of the public: It was a horse drawn society and horses did not take kindly to encountering these noisy, smelly, leviathans invading their hitherto untroubled world. Horses could, and did, rear and bolt, injuring both their passengers and pedestrians.

To sabotage these unwelcome intruders, piles of stones would be placed on the roads in an attempt to break axles as they came round a bend.

The worst blow, however, was Turnpike charges: On the Liverpool run, for example, the charge for a horse drawn coach was four shillings but for a steam coach, two pounds eight shillings. So the horse lobby, the public, the railways, the Turnpikes were all attempting, with ultimately great success, to make steam coaches unviable.

It also must be appreciated that despite excellent technical progress the Steam carriage, at that stage, was not really developed enough to take over the roads. The steering problem, for example, had not yet been solved.

Horse drawn carriages had power steering: Horse power! The horses between the shafts turned the vehicle without trouble but without the horses, steering the steam coaches presented a formidable challenge.

Various methods were tried: Gurney tried to replace the leverage provided by horses by having a beam projecting from the fore carriage and at the front of this beam a pair of small wheels controlled by a tiller with a seat for the steersman: Not the most practical of arrangements!

Hancock used a pedal operated steering damper to control yawing but it did nothing to compensate for the lack of the leverage provided by the horses.

Finally the roads themselves were nothing like ready to take these necessarily heavy vehicles, weighing between three and five tons. Tarmac had not been invented and although roadbuilding had advanced considerably, maintenance hadn't and potholes were a formidable hazard. The problem of the roads with their neglected and unsuitable surfaces was to face the first motor cars when they emerged over half a century later.

But what about the internal combustion engine which was to be essential to provide a lightweight power unit if the embryo cars and motorcycles were to be successful?

The first successful motorcar was the Benz which took to the road in Mannheim in 1886 but many decades of progress and endeavour had to come first.

It had been demonstrated, before 1800, that a hydrogen/air mixture could be ignited by an electric spark and as early as 1784 a man named Street produced a specification for an "explosion engine" described as follows: "The explosion was to be caused by vaporising spirits of turpentine on a heated metal surface, mixing the vapour with air in a cylinder, firing the mixture and driving a piston by the explosion produced." But there is no evidence that such an engine was actually produced.

In 1807 a Frenchman, De Rivaz is reported to have propelled a vehicle by an engine fuelled by a hydrogen/ air mixture fired by an electric spark and by 1825 Samuel Butler of Brompton had produced and sold some of his "Gas vacuum engines" probably using the same system.

The burning of sulphuretted hydrogen was used to create a vacuum in a cylinder and then atmospheric pressure drove the piston as in the earliest steam engines. These engines undoubtedly worked and one was fitted to a vehicle which climbed Shooter's Hill, Blackheath, without trouble.

An enormous amount of experimental work was carried out throughout the nineteenth century on attempting to design and make successful internal combustion engines but their work has gone unrecorded and is long forgotten.

At Fletcher's, for example, old timers assured me that designs from the 1860's for an internal combustion engine by George Fletcher still survived in the drawing office archives. The engine was designed to run on a powdered coal/air mixture. Much to my regret I never had the opportunity to search for these ancient drawings.

Lenoir made the first practical internal combustion engine in 1860: It had a single stroke cycle with an engine configuration like a double acting steam engine. A charge of uncompressed gas/air mixture was drawn in by the piston and halfway down the stroke the mixture was fired by electric spark to drive the piston down to the bottom of the stroke. The returning piston ejected the exhaust gas and on the opposite side of the piston the similar cycle was operating.

Lenoir's engines were manufactured and sold, despite their inefficiency. They were stationary engines running on gas but in his patent specification he described a surface vaporiser to be warmed by the exhaust to enable the engine to burn liquid fuel. In 1862 one of these engines adapted to run on liquid fuel was fitted into a vehicle and ran from Paris to Joinville-le-Pont a number of times though the six mile journey was said to have taken two or three hours.

Compressing the charge before ignition was proposed by Barnett as early as 1838 but it was not until Beau de Rochas outlined the four stroke cycle in 1862 that its importance was realised and finally patented and put into practical effect a few years later by Otto.

The first commercially successful stationary engines working on the four stroke cycle were made by Gottlieb Daimler in 1872 and patented by Otto and Daimler in 1876. These engines worked on the same lines as all four stroke engines made today. The engines were named the "Otto silent gas engine" though "silent" was an optimistic description!

A puzzling episode in the search for the first motorcar is to be found in the work of Siegfried Marcus in Vienna. Starting in 1870 he built four motorcars and one, reputedly built in 1873, still survives.

Although the vehicle is crude the engine is immensely interesting: It is a single cylinder with mechanically operated valves and a low tension magneto, anticipating the work of Frederick Simms some twenty years later. It has a peculiar carburettor, warmed by the exhaust and the spray of petrol is provided by a revolving brush.

This amazing survival was overhauled in 1950 and was found to run satisfactorily, so was this the first motorcar? Perhaps so, but the first man to design and produce a car for sale to the public was Karl Benz in 1886.

Finally by 1880 engines were being developed to run on petroleum spirit or gasoline. "Petrol" was a proprietary name, coined by London importers.

Gottleib Daimler and Karl Benz were working on engines specifically for motor vehicles and they both had petrol powered road vehicles, of a sort, running in 1885. Benz's vehicle was a tricycle, Daimler's a bicycle and although they both lived quite near each other in Germany neither knew of the other's work. Daimler, however, did not continue with an improved motor car but concentrated on engines for motor boats and light machinery.

Benz continued with the development of a road vehicle and completed a successful single cylinder engine with belt operated two speed gear, surface carburettor and spark ignition. Final drive was by chain through a differential.

So with the arrival of the Benz in 1886, a recognisable and practical motorcar, the age of motoring had arrived and, on the Continent, development continued.

In England, however, the legal brakes were still locked on! The 1861 Act was still in force with the speed of mechanically propelled vehicles still restricted to 2mph in town and 4mph in the country. In 1878 the red flag requirement had been dropped though the requirement for a footman in front still applied but now only having to walk twenty yards ahead.

In November 1896, however, the breakthrough came at last and the overall speed limit was raised to 14mph though immediately reduced by the Local Government Board to 12mph. In 1903 the limit was raised to a dizzy 20mph.

By November 1896, then, the curtain had been raised and the show was about to begin. Embryo cars and motorcycles were both on the road and under frantic development. Nothing would ever be the same again.

But up until 1914 cars were very much rich men's toys and, to a lesser extent, so were motorcycles. Ixion, the motorcycling writer and pioneer motorcyclist estimated that there were only as little as twenty privately owned motorcycles in Great Britain in 1900. He bought his first motorcycle in 1901 and did not know a single private owner of a motorcycle in the large county in which he lived and within a radius of fifty miles he only knew of three owners of motor cars. All wealthy men who regarded their vehicles as scientific toys rather than serious modes of transport.

In 1900 there was not one square yard of tarmac on British roads so on a summer day a large car of the period could raise a cloud of dust a mile long and twenty feet high. The dust could linger for up to an hour. In wet weather the car and motorcycle travelled in a stream of liquid filth, a mixture of mud and animal droppings. In the case of the motorcyclist this filth penetrated every article of clothing.

The motorist and motorcyclist were objects of hatred for nearly everyone: These noisy, smelly, unfamiliar monsters terrified horses to the fury of their unfortunate owners. The mildest of dobbins pulling the farmer's trap could turn into a rodeo act when encountering a car.

The way was open at last for powered road transport. Open it may well have been but the way ahead was far from clear. For a start these new vehicles had to travel on roads and the roads of the day were totally unsuitable.

Road surfaces were constructed of two inch stones packed with mud and compacted by a steam roller, but since the 1840's the maintenance of roads had been a very low priority. Iron shod cart wheels, iron horseshoes, combined with the erosion of rain, snow and frost soon damaged the road surface which then disintegrated into a series of potholes. Some of these potholes were so deep that when the front wheel of an early motorcycle dropped into them the machine was brought to a sickening halt and the rider thrown over the handlebars. Cars, too, suffered almost as badly.

The opposition to the steam coaches fifty years before was now directed against the motoring and motorcycling fraternity. The early steamers had been halted but attempts to halt the motoring age were merely swimming against the tide.

Even so, the opposition did all it could. The chief weapon against the steamers had been the high turnpike charges but the turnpike system had long gone so that weapon could not be used again. The horse owning fraternity and the local magistrates were all against the motorists who got short shrift from the Bench who ensured that the Police watched motorists like hawks to catch them speeding. With a speed limit of 12 mph this was not going to be difficult.

A constable with a stop watch would be stationed at one point and another a mile distant. Any unfortunate motorist or motorcyclist speeding at over 12 mph would be prosecuted and would receive no mercy. The evidence of the police was unchallengable. One policeman stopped a motorist in Brighton and gave his estimated speed as 153mph (I do like that extra 3 mph!)

The roads out of London and many big towns were happy hunting grounds for police speed traps and it was not until the AA engaged the services of an eminent Counsel to study the problem and become an expert in the use of stop watches, that some relief was obtained. He was able to demonstrate, in a series of Court actions, that such evidence was subject to many errors.

In 1903 the speed limit was raised to 20 mph but far from reducing police persecution, it became even worse! Eventually, of course, the magistrates themselves and the landed gentry started to take up this new form of transport so the persecution eased at last.

This 20mph speed limit continued through the 1920's, though universally ignored, until all speed limits were abolished in 1930.

In 1934 a 30mph speed limit was brought in for built up areas and at the same time, driving tests for learner drivers were introduced.

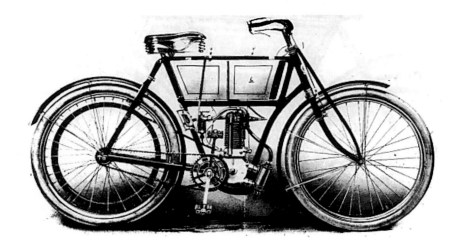

(Top) De Dion-Bouton twin cylinder car price £446. This is how the
motor car had evolved by 1903. The De-Dions were well built
practical cars and reliable, too, by the standards of their day.
De-Dion engines were also used in a number of other makes with
their single cylinder engines used in motorcycles.
(Left) New Hudson motorcycle price £45. This is how
motorcycles had evolved by 1903. This had a 350cc engine and
the drive was by belt from the engine to rear wheel with no
gearbox or clutch. Forks were unsprung and the pedals provided
LPA (light pedal assistance) on hills!

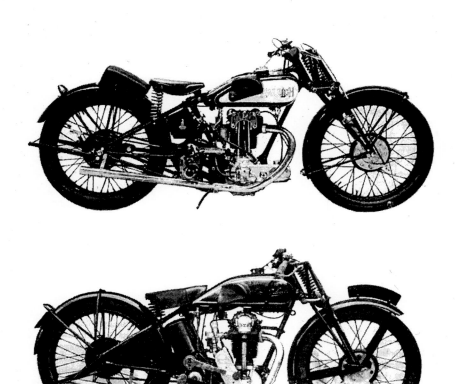

(Top) 1930 350cc T.T. Raleigh. Looking old fashioned for 1930 but one finished fifth in the Junior T.T. of that year. Six years later, Alf Briggs of Derby, riding an identical one, won the Folbigg Trophy at Cadwell Park for the fastest eight laps of the year. This machine was superbly restored by Alf.

(Bottom) 1930 Velocette 350cc KTT overhead camshaft production racer. Surely the most successful 350 production racer of all time. The "Works" Velocette racers challenged the Norton supremacy throughout the late 1920's and 1930's.

Chapter Eighteen
Outstanding
Derbyshire Motorcyclists

Derby and Derbyshire have produced some remarkable motorcyclists and by this I mean truly remarkable without the inverted commas! One of the most outstanding is Alf Briggs. Not only is Alf an outstanding rider but a superb motorcycle engineer and tuner.

Alf could get the utmost out of any motorcycle in both performance and handling: During the 1930's Alf was the man to beat in short circuit road racing, trials, grasstrack and scrambles. His wife Molly, too, was no mean twistgrip tweaker, riding competitively in many of those branches of motorcycle sport. She rode a 350 Tiger 80 Triumph in grasstracks, trials and scrambles and after the War shoehorned into it a 500 all alloy Triumph Trophy engine which she continued to campaign successfully. First class motorcycle mechanic, too, maintaining and repairing motorcycles for the Fire Service during the War.

Alf's was brilliantly successful at Cadwell Park and his performance on the road circuit there had to be seen to be believed.

Raleigh motorcycles were "local" in that they were made in nearby Nottingham but it is not a marque that springs to mind when road racing is being discussed. Even so, though never among the winners, they did build racing models and ran them in the T.T. They entered a 350 in the 1922 T.T. but it failed to finish. There was then a gap until they tried in earnest in 1928.

These 1928 racers were based on standard machines, modified for racing. The 500cc models had their gearboxes laid on their sides to achieve a shorter wheelbase. Two retired, due to unfortunate incidents: One lost its carburettor jets, another lost its tyre valve, though a final machine finished eighth, and in the Junior event one finished seventh, so that was a start! For the next year, however, a 500 finished 15th and all 350's retired.

For 1930 they started to get their skates on with the 500cc models reputed to be capable of 100 mph. C.J Williams was fifth in the Junior and Johnny Duncan 10th in the Senior. In addition they won the Austrian T.T. and achieved third place in the Belgian T.T.

For 1931 they really tried with redesigned 350 and 500 engines. They had electron (magnesium alloy) crankcases, downdraught inlet ports and dry sump lubrication with a complicated system of external oil pumps. As well as the complex oil-pump, dry-sump engines for the T.T., they had also made simpler total loss oiling machines for short circuits.

These T.T. 500's were reputedly the fastest on the Island, timed at 112mph at Hilberry, though this was probably the last time that a British manufacturer designed 500cc racing motorcycle engines with pushrod overhead valves when overhead camshafts had clearly taken the lead. The results, however, were disappointing with Arthur Tyler achieving seventh place in the Senior. Best Junior position was twenty first. Arthur Tyler, however, never lost his interest in motorcycles and only died recently in late 1998 aged 89.

That, as far as Raleigh was concerned, was the end of the line for racing and about three years later they ceased production of motorcycles altogether.

So that was the end of the special Raleigh racing motorcycles, wasn't it? Wasn't it?

No it wasn't! Alf Briggs obtained one of the out-dated 1930 350's and set to work! Alf really made this machine fly and raced it successfully at Cadwell against more modern overhead camshaft Nortons and Velocettes. The premier award at Cadwell was the Folbigg Trophy, won by the rider who achieved the fastest eight laps of the year.

In 1936 Alf was racing his 350 at Cadwell, accompanied by his "racing mechanic", Derby butcher Harry Domleo. Harry was a fellow enthusiast who rode 350 Velocettes. In Alf's heat the Raleigh seized on the line: It had the alcohol barrel and piston fitted for maximum performance but Alf had with him the lower compression petrol/benzol barrel and piston.

Alf and Harry worked frantically to change over to the petrol/benzol set-up and with one minute to go to the start of the final they still hadn't finished! Amazingly, however, the machine was on the line for the start of the final and Alf shot away like the proverbial scalded cat! By now it had started to rain but despite the rain and slower petrol/benzol engine Alf achieved the fastest eight laps of the year to win the Folbigg Trophy. An amazing achievement with an engine that was not only out of date then but was even out of date at the time it was designed and surely one of Cadwell's most outstanding rides.

Alf eventually sold this 350 to Chris Harrison in 1938 for Chris to use in Grass Track racing but, as far as is known, it has not survived. Alf still has an identical model, however, and although nothing is known of its T.T. history it is the actual machine that won the first ever event at Donington Park and tied for first place in the 1,000cc class. He also has the 1931 500 that Arthur Tyler rode into seventh place in the 1931 T.T.. Alf has restored them both to pristine condition.

In the late 1930's Alf and his wife rode in Grass Track or short circuit road races practically every weekend in the season. They rode all over the country ending up with Triumph Tiger 80's and a 1938 Triumph Speed Twin which Alf tuned and fitted with twin carburettors.

For Transport they had an elderly Daimler limousine which cost them £15. One machine went inside and the other was fastened on the running board. It had the Daimler double sleeve valve engine which, by then, was well worn and consumed oil at a prodigious rate. They drove it down to the Hampshire Grand National, in which they were riding, taking with them a five gallon drum of oil to slake the engine's insatiable thirst. It was almost enough .... they only had to buy an extra gallon on the way home!

Although Alf bought the two Raleigh racers from different owners in different parts of the country there was a strange similarity: In both cases he went to see the machines and the purchase was agreed but as he was starting to load them up, both owners changed their minds and decided not to sell after all! It took further hours of discussion before he was finally allowed to take them away.

A more straightforward purchase was a humble 1929 250 sidevalve Raleigh that had lain unused for years only a few streets away until Alf was asked if he would like to buy it. He restored this, too, and added it to his collection.

Alf joined Honda as their technical service expert when they first came to the UK and then moved from motorcycles to cars, remaining as a consultant until he was eighty years old and becoming a personal friend of Sochiro Honda. At 84 years old he still drives a car, Honda, of course, and remains as mentally alert as ever.

I managed to acquire one of the 1931 350 T.T. Raleigh engines after the War and fitted it into my Speedway Rudge. Now to powerslide a speedway machine you must have power and we wondered if the 350 Raleigh would be up to it? We need not have worried: The 350 went like the proverbial bomb and when you hurtled into a bend, laid the machine over and wound open the throttle, the machine slid beautifully. I still have the engine... but not the rest of the bike to go with it!

Another outstanding Derby motorcyclist was Michael McEvoy. He manufactured motorcycles at Leaper Street. Derby in the maze of streets behind Kedleston Road. Although only in motorcycle production for a few years, McEvoy machines made a surprising impact on the motorcycle world.

They made all sorts of models with all kinds of engines from small Villiers two-strokes to 1000cc British Anzani and J.A.P. vee-twins. It is for the big twins that they are best remembered with beautifully designed duplex frames when this type of construction was most unusual and ahead of its time. Riding one of these big twin McEvoys in his student days so impressed Phil Vincent that he was inspired to finally design his own immortal Vincent vee-twin.

George Pagett, who was to go on to a successful career in the world of motorcycle manufacture and C. Archie Birkin, brother of Sir Henry Birkin of Bentley fame, were both associated with McEvoy's. George rode the big vee-twins at Brooklands and was the only man to ride McEvoys in the T.T. This was in 1926 when he rode a 350, which he had curiously named the "Sea pig", into 28th place but failed to finish on a 500. He wrote a series of articles in the motorcycle magazines in the 1940's describing his experiences on his 1,000cc McEvoy which he named "Rumbethump", not a bad description for the powerful uneven beat of a big vee-twin.

When his days with the big McEvoy were over he sawed the frame into small pieces so that no-one else would ever be able to ride it. This was a sad end for one of the great classic motorcycles as very few can have survived.

Stan Burnett rode a 1,000cc McEvoy on the road that had been raced at Brooklands by George Pagett and later fitted it with a brand new 1,000cc J.A.P. vee-twin racing engine. These engines were designed to run on alcohol with two Speedway J.A.P. top halves on a common crankcase. As engines running on alcohol run much cooler the cylinder barrels and heads have only skimpy finning. Carburation was by two racing Amal carburettors, each with twin float chambers.

Power output was 78BHP and to put this into perspective, the works 500 Norton that won the 1938 T.T. produced 49 BHP, the difference being that as the big J.A.P. was two speedway engines combined the power was instantly on tap whereas the Norton did not come on song until the revs were high enough to get it "on the megaphone".

We bought this machine from Stan after the war and riding it on the road, illegally, of course, on alcohol, was an unforgettable experience: Nothing before had prepared us for the sheer brute power of this monster. You had to change up with care or the front wheel would be up in the air.

I wonder if it has survived and what happened to its original 1927 1,000 cc J.A.P. engine. No doubt Stan sold it, at the time, for a few pounds.

Michael McEvoy was a larger than life character and bon viveur. He would disappear for weeks at a time onto the Continent with his girlfriend, later his wife, Jimmy Simpson's sister. Jimmy was the legendary T.T. rider.

Jimmy Simpson was known as "Hard luck Simpson" because although he was a brilliant rider who was the first man to lap the T.T. course at 60, 70 and 80mph the bikes of those days didn't stand up to Jimmy's hard riding and often blew up! He rode in twenty six T.T.'s from 1922, made eight fastest laps but only finished in eleven. His last year was 1934 and he went out in a blaze of glory: Second in the Senior and Junior, both on Nortons and first in the Lightweight on one of the legendary four valve Rudges.

Although McEvoys were never famous for T.T. successes they were ridden successfully at Brooklands by Michael McEvoy, George Pagett and others. In the early thirties they gave up motorcycle manufacture and went into the production of superchargers for sports cars.

Michael McEvoy went on to serve in the War, ending up as a Major. After the War he was stationed in Germany, then exhausted and devastated by bombing and it is accepted that it was largely due to his energy and initiative that Volkswagen production was eventually started again.

Freddie Hatton was a 1920's racing man who rode New Hudson's solo and Douglas sidecars in the T.T. My Aunt Edna knew him and remembers seeing him prepare his racing Douglas engines, cleaning everything finally in a first and second paraffin bath. He had a motorcycle business in London Road Derby in the late 1920's but this, like so many others, closed about 1930 and Freddie moved to the Birmingham area where he went on both to sell cars and race them.

Although not a Derby man, the great racing motorcyclist, "Ginger" Wood, (not to be confused with Stanley Woods), was based at Derby during the War as the S.U. carburettor expert on Rolls Royce aero engines and after the war he was called in as a consultant when Triumph fitted S.U. carburettors to their 650 Thunderbirds. During the time when he was based at Rolls Royce, Derby, he stayed with Stan Burnett's family.

Ginger Wood had raced in the T.T. and at Brooklands throughout the 1930's and was the first man to cover 100 miles in one hour on a twin cylinder machine at Brooklands. This means to keep it up for an hour, not merely to hit 100mph for a short period.

In the 1930's New Imperial made very successful racing 250's, winning the Lightweight T.T. with one in 1936. They made a 500cc racer by mounting two barrels and heads of the 250's on a common crankcase and this was the machine elected to attempt the 100mph hour record at Brooklands in 1934.

The New Imp 500 took some riding: Handling was notoriously eccentric and the front cylinder had a tendency to oil up at high revs. Les Archer had agreed with Ginger a series of pit signals: Arms outstretched meant that the speed was being maintained. Arms at his side meant that the speed was dropping. Arms above his head meant "Too fast, slow down".

So all was set for the attempt on the record but there was a small problem: While waiting for the machine to be finally prepared in Birmingham, Ginger took a Velocette for a trial run which Noel Christmas had been tuning. Ginger was riding it along a road nearby when, without warning, a car turned across the road in front of him and Ginger slid down the road, tearing the skin off his back. Only ten days to go so Ginger got bandaged up and hoped for the best. He needed the job so he said nothing to New Imperials.

Halfway through the attempt two things happened: Firstly he forgot which pit signal was which and secondly the scab on his back came adrift! The machine went round with power to spare and averaged over 102mph for the hour.

In 1935 riding a further improved version he raised the lap record to 115.82mph.

Although much work was put into the 500 twin, both on engine and frame, it was never really successful and handling problems were never finally solved. Ginger rode it in the 1935 and 1936 T.T.'s but it failed to finish both times and after 1936 New Imperials gave up racing though 250 production racers were still produced and sold.

It was by no means the end of the line for racing as far as Ginger was concerned, however. One of the most outstanding 250's of the late thirties was the Excelsior Manxman. They were made in production and racing form. Attractive, cobby machines that looked if they were straining to go even when standing still.

Overhead camshaft engines in classic style. They were introduced in 1935 and in 1936 they really came into their own.

In the 1936 Lightweight T.T., riding an Excelsior Manxman, Ginger failed to finish but in 1937 he almost made it! He was beaten into second place by a mere 37 seconds by Omobono Tenni on the works Guzzi.

He went on to be placed in several classic road races and in 1938 he was again second in the Lightweight T.T. behind Ewald Kluge on the ear splitting supercharged 250 D.K.W. with other Excelsior's third, fourth, fifth, sixth, seventh and ninth!

For 1939 Ginger rode one of the amazing home-tuned Pike Rudges in the Lightweight, a Velocette in the Junior and a Norton in the Senior and although not among the winners he was not disgraced.

The American President Taft was a man of few words: So much so that he was practically silent. One evening, at a dinner party, he was seated next to a beautiful girl: Turning to the President she said brightly "I have taken a bet, Mr President, that tonight I will get more than two words out of you". "You lose" replied the President!

At last I met up with Ginger Wood at the end of the War: I was a red-hot motorcycle enthusiast and a trained engineer. Ginger was one of the all time motorcycle greats who had been everywhere, done everything. There was much to discuss.

So how did I get on? I didn't! That young lady got more out of President Taft than I got out of Ginger on motorcycling! I found this strange, even baffling, because most motorcyclists or ex-motorcyclists are only too pleased to talk motorcycles. I was, however, to find out later that this was Ginger's way. He did *not* talk motorcycles other than to a favoured few.... and, to paraphrase Sam Goldwyn, Ginger included me out!

Denis Jones of Long Eaton is a fantastically talented engineer who designed and built motorcycle frames and engines. Four cylinder engines are commonplace today but not so in the 1930's yet Denis, as a private venture, designed and built several. One was a four cylinder supercharged two-stroke and he also built four-cylinder overhead camshaft engines and single cylinder 250cc twin cam engines.

He designed all these engines from scratch from scratch and drew them on a drawing board. He then made wooden patterns for the aluminium castings and when the castings were made he did all the machining. Even pistons were made in the same way. All the engine internals .... crankshafts, camshafts, etc. he made on his lathe.

He designed and made the frames and forks and on some models he even made the hubs and brakes.

When I expressed amazement at such skill, enterprise and dedication, Denis said "Anyone could do it!" But, as you know full well, they certainly could not! Engineers of Denis' calibre are as scarce as cardboard camshafts!

Finally in 1998 Denis was left with only one of his creations, the four cylinder supercharged two-stroke. An enthusiast owned two of his machines, a 250 and an overhead camshaft four-cylinder and he finally persuaded Denis to sell him the supercharged four-cylinder two-stroke. Shortly after acquiring it he sold the lot for £35,000 .... each!

Denis eventually specialised in a business modifying cars for disabled people, displaying endless ingenuity to enable people without a chance of personal mobility to drive again. On one occasion he was asked if he could modify a car for a woman with no arms and a club foot to drive: Denis did it!

So Denis is another "hands on" engineer prepared to accept any challenge and proof again that: "Once a motorcyclist, always a motorcyclist".

Laurie Fletcher of Quarndon has owned seven motorcycles in his career and every one was a "Camshaft Veller". His first was bought for £8 from Charlie Gatenby's father. The Gatenbys, father and son, were lifelong motorcycle enthusiasts. Laurie sold it later for £4. He has owned two KTT's, a Mark IV that had been owned by the legendary T.T. and Brooklands rider, Les Archer and a Mark VI. For many years now he has been a talented aero-engine model maker, aero-engine collector and unofficial Rolls Royce aero-engine historian.

Collecting aero-engines is not like collecting classic watches or even motorcycles: Not only are they big, but heavy and unwieldy. Not that any of that deters Laurie: If he is unable to obtain the original he makes a model and his models are superb.

During the War Rolls Royce designed a forty eight cylinder engine with two plugs per cylinder...ninety six sparking plugs. None were ever made but the drawings exist and Laurie has made a model.

In World War One as well as conventional in line water-cooled aero-engines, rotary engines were made that were remarkably efficient with power to weight ratio often better than the in line models. In the rotary engines the crankshaft stood still and the propeller was bolted to the crankcase that spun round; sounds odd to us today but they did work and worked well. Rotaries are not thick on the ground these days but in 1916 a rotary engined plane crashed in the Humber Estuary and a few years ago the dredge of a fishing boat hit the wreckage. The remains of the Clerget rotary engine were brought up and ended up with Laurie who will, eventually, rebuild it.

Derrick Bedwell is a lifelong motorcyclist and ex Rolls Royce man. During the War he was appointed "Trouble-shooter" to Lancaster Squadrons. Derrick, in his time, has owned about a dozen KTT Velocettes of various marks ending up with the latest of all, the Mark VIII. He has also owned as many Manx Nortons.

He would turn up at an airfield on his Manx Norton and ask if there were any motorcycle enthusiasts there. The answer, of course, was always "Yes". "Right." Derrick would say "We will hold a meeting in the Sergeants' Mess in two days time". That evening all the enthusiasts would turn up and the topic was motorcycles, motorcycles, motorcycles!

On one occasion Derrick was kind enough to lend a fellow enthusiast a van and a K.T.T. Velocette on the understanding that he would maintain them both. Van and Velo then disappeared from human ken! About a year later a friend of Derrick's, who knew the van, saw it broken down near Burton. He raced to tell Derrick who hurtled out there. He found the man, van and Velo so was reunited with his property at last, vividly bringing home to him the wisdom of Bill Shakespeare's statement "Neither a borrower or a lender be".

There were, and still are, many other outstanding motorcycle enthusiasts and talented engineers in Derby and district, far too many to mention here.

a simple stirrup brake working on the rim like a push bike. The A.B.C., however, had internal expanding brakes on both wheels.

It also had electric lighting with a battery charged by a dynamo, surely a British "first" when acetylene lighting was universal.

In the early days of motorcycling the frames were little more than heavier push bike frames. The single down tube came down from the steering head but in place of the cycle's bottom bracket, the engine was fitted. This was the traditional "single down tube" frame which continues in use today, particularly for lightweight motorcycles.

The A.B.C. was one of the first to use the duplex frame. Granville Bradshaw kept his horizontally opposed twin engine, mounted across the frame, as narrow as possible using an "oversquare" design i.e. with the stroke shorter than the width of the bore... a breakthrough at the time when longstroke engines were the vogue. The opposed cylinders were tucked inside the duplex frame tubes, acting as built in crash bars in the event of an accident.

The "duplex" frame means that instead of a single downtube, there are a pair of tubes, coming down from the steering head and usually sweeping under the engine, at either side, and ending at each side of the rear wheel spindle. In the days of rigid frames and dodgy handling, the duplex frame was a great improvement. The frame was sprung front and rear and the design included built in legshields and undertray. This engine/gearbox layout preceded B.M.W. by four years and was surely the inspiration for it.

Immediately after the War, Sopwith was searching for a project to keep his aircraft factory going and decided on the A.B.C.. The factory was inundated with orders but there were problems! Production was delayed due to a number of factors, the price shot up from an estimated £70 to a shocking £160 and when the machines did appear they were dogged by troubles.

Had more time been taken on development these troubles would have been easily eliminated: For example the overhead rockers were lubricated by squirting with an oil can, a method that proved hopelessly inadequate, but despite all the snags it was one of the greatest evolutionary designs of all time. Unfortunately modifications came too late and the Company failed.

Motorcyclists, however, continued to ride them for years and proprietary oil systems were designed and sold to solve the overhead rocker gear oiling problem. They also made their mark at Brooklands and were the first motorcycles to use megaphone exhaust systems in the T.T., though none finished!

Immediately after World War One there was a short-lived scooter boom. These early scooters had no seat and you stood on the footboard as with a child's scooter. The engines were mounted above the front wheel which did not enhance stability or safety.

They were American imports and sold like hot cakes. Granville Bradshaw seized the opportunity with his hastily designed Scootamota which, unlike many of its competitors, had a saddle and at £40 outsold all its rivals.

Unfortunately the time was not ripe for scooters and would not be so for another quarter of a century or more. Napoleon said "An invention before its time is never appreciated" and although he hadn't really got scooters in his mind it equally applied to them. These rudimentary designs bristled with defects and this soon became obvious. The wet summer of 1920 and the disadvantages of inflation brought the scooter boom to an end.

(Top) Me on the 1927 680cc vee-twin sidevalve New Imperial. It ran very well despite sounding like a circular saw!
(Bottom) T on his well kept original 1936 350cc ohv Ariel, bought for £25. A typical mid-thirties overhead valver, stylish and with excellent performance.
(Left) The imaginative 1928 Ascot Pullin designed by the brilliant engineer Dougal Marchant. Although produced and sold, it soon failed as it was just too far ahead of its time.

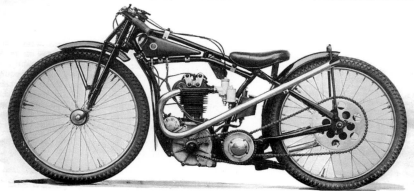

(Top) In the early days of Speedway the Douglas led the field and leg trailing was the style.

(Bottom) The all conquering Speedway Rudge that vanquished the Douglases when it was introduced in 1930. Four-valve engine running on alcohol and much shorter wheelbase. Although the alcohol J.A.P. engines were to finally supersede the Rudges, the basic Rudge frame design was to continue as the Martin J.A.P., often simply called the Speedway J.A.P..

Chapter Twenty
Grass Track Racing

On August Monday 1944 Grass Track races were to be held at Radcliffe-on-Trent near Nottingham. There was no private motoring so alcohol fuel was to be used. This was the ideal opportunity to give our grasstrack Velocette an airing. It was already prepared, now all we had to do was to find some fuel. The answer was methylated spirits but due to shortages you could only get a few ounces from each chemist so we went the rounds slowly getting a supply together. To get our machines to the meeting we had to go by train from the now closed L.N.E.R. station at Friargate, Derby. About half a dozen of us from Derby pushed our machines to the station and loaded them into the Guard's Van. Once at Radcliffe on Trent we pushed our machines to the meeting.

All sorts of odd and unlikely machines had been entered for the meeting but some superlative ones as well. One professional speedway rider, A.F.Elliott, turned up with his Speedway J.A.P. and local enthusiast Stan Burnett had his home tuned 1930 Speedway Rudge. The only other Speedway J.A.P. was ridden by motorcycle fanatic and RAF pilot, Dixon Spain.

A number of Nottingham enthusiasts had turned up and we knew them all: Among them were Sam Pearce, the Scott enthusiast, though Velocette mounted for this meeting. Fron Purslow on an incredibly noisy International Norton and A.A.W. (Bill) Myers, the leader of the pack, also riding a Velocette.

Among riders from elsewhere were Derek Bedwell, RR Merlin expert and trouble-shooter to Lancaster Squadrons on his highly tuned 500 Ariel. A.R. Ellison who rode his 350 Tiger 80 Triumph brilliantly. Ron Carvill of Coventry, another first class rider on a 350 Grass Track Special O.K. Supreme. Alf Briggs, one of Derby's most talented riders. Len Tupling on his home tuned "Tupling Special" that went like a bomb! Was it a 1920's "Big Port" A.J.S. or a 350 four-valve Rudge?

A "mystery" rider was P. Goodman of Derby on a 350 Velocette who also entered a later grasstrack meeting as P. Goodman of Birmingham. This was none other than Peter Goodman, son of the Goodmans who manufactured Velocettes and the machine he was riding was borrowed from Alf Briggs.

Peter was a brilliant rider whose racing career had been interrupted by the War. He was to ride successfully after the war achieving third place in the Senior T.T. of 1947 and fourth place in the Junior riding pre- war Works Velocettes. This was his only T.T. ride as shortly after, when leading in a race at Strasbourg, he collided with a marshal who had ventured onto the circuit to retrieve a piece of debris and was very severely injured. This, unfortunately, ended his racing career, though after the War he was to continue in the family firm, eventually becoming Works Director.

Strangely enough Alf Briggs was hit by another rider on the same day but in a Midlands Grass Track meeting and suffered near fatal injuries, though he was eventually to resume racing again.

During the War Alf ran a machine shop turning out War material and Peter Goodman was an RAF Aircrew member, flying from Ashbourne Aerodrome near Derby. As they were fellow motorcycle enthusiasts they eventually met and got together. Peter was riding a strange all-black machine from the aerodrome to his home in Birmingham when on leave and he gave Alf a ride on it: It was the one-off hand built prototype of the revolutionary 150cc water cooled twin LE Velocette, the machine designed to capture that lucrative, but always elusive, "Everyman" market.

Now Stan Burnett, like Chris Harrison, was a Rolls Royce man and a born engineer. A brilliant rider, too, whose powerslides were incomparable and no-one could slide 'em like Stan Burnett. He had worked on his 500 Speedway Rudge engine and persuaded it to produce enough power to challenge the much more up to date

148

Speedway J.A.P. engines. In the 500cc final Stan gave a performance I will never forget. Stan and the Speedway professional, Elliot, came round the final bend together in a full lock slide, shoulder to shoulder and this is not merely a figure of speech...... They were touching shoulders with each man straining against the other. They crossed the finishing line side by side, but the moral victory was Stan's.

His next grasstrack project was an early 30's 500 A.J.S. with chain-driven overhead camshaft. He rebuilt that engine, too, persuading it to produce the kind of power that would have astonished its designer and, in addition, he shortened the wheelbase by bending the front downtube and cranking the rear chainstays. He ended up with a fearsome performer that went like a bomb!

A young RAF man had turned up hoping to borrow a bike to ride and at the end of the planned racing a makeshift "mountain" course was laid out with a hillside in the park acting as the mountain section. He had borrowed a bike for this and came down the steep downhill section with me close behind him. At the bottom his bike slewed sideways and I had no choice but to hit his machine. Fortunately neither of us was hurt but I did rip the shirt off his back! The rider? None other than Eric Oliver who was to go on to become World Sidecar Champion.

So did I clean up in the 350 class with my Velocette? Unfortunately not, but I did ride with great enthusiasm and thoroughly enjoyed myself.

After that first meeting other events were held round the Midlands in 1945 and I was a regular performer, always going by train and pushing my bike to the public park where the meeting was held. For the 500cc class I bought a Speedway Rudge of early thirties vintage. No brakes and no gearbox, just a countershaft with clutch, but how those bikes could go! High compression engines running on alcohol.

Stan later bought a Speedway J.A.P. engine for his Rudge and I bought his home tuned Speedway Rudge engine with its remarkable boost in performance. I was later to fit Speedway J.A.P. engines to my machine, first an excellent four stud engine then a brand new later five stud engine.

149

My final step was the purchase of a pukka Speedway J.A.P. that had been raced at Nottingham Speedway in the late 1930's by Freddie Strekker.

The Speedway J.A.P.'s had no brakes and no gearbox, just a countershaft with clutch. The engines had a fourteen and a half to one compression ratio compared to about seven to one for a normal sports motorcycle running on petrol and the power was unbelievable.... ideal for the powerslides so necessary in Grasstrack or Speedway.

To powerslide a motorcycle is one of the most exhilarating forms of motion known to man: You hurtle into a bend at a speed far higher than you can possibly get round but as you enter the bend you lay the machine hard over and open the throttle. The rear wheel then spins under power and swings outwards and this is the tricky bit! Just keep the throttle open and the bike would spin out of control. Shut off and the rear wheel would bite, throwing you off. The trick is to juggle the throttle to keep the bike sliding yet under control. At the same time the front wheel comes upright and is turned hard into the direction of the slide. Absolutely exhilarating when you master the technique.

So in a powerslide the machine is travelling faster than if ridden round in the normal way and a skilled Speedway rider has to not merely keep the machine sliding and under control, but to manoeuvre for position among his fellow competitors who are sliding side by side with him and doing the same thing!

I thoroughly enjoyed Grasstrack Racing though unlike Stan, who could have made it to the very top in either Grasstrack or Speedway, I was never among the winners. After the War Stan did ride as a Speedway professional for a time but the only transport was by train as there was no petrol for van or trailer. To ride at Glasgow, for example, was a feat of endurance for only a modest sum of money and after a similar trip to Norwich, Stan realised that as a budding entrepreneur he had bigger fish to fry.

During the War Matchless had introduced their "Teledraulic" front fork. This was a hydraulically damped telescopic fork and a vast improvement on the girder forks it replaced. It was every motorcyclist's ambition to have one but, of course, none were available.

At Chilwell near Long Eaton there was a huge Army depot and among their many duties they rebuilt crash damaged Army motorcycles. Matchlesses with Teledraulic forks would be sent there for repair and if the forks were badly bent they would simply be scrapped and new forks fitted. No time available to fiddle about rebuilding damaged forks. The old forks were loaded onto railway trucks and sent for scrap, but if only we could lay our hands on that scrap!

Impossible, you would have thought, but Stan found a way and a supply of damaged forks ended up in his hands. Stan rebuilt them and we all fitted Stan's Matchless Teledraulics to our machines with a vast improvement in comfort and handling. The snag, of course, was that those girder forks we discarded are irreplaceable today when the bikes of that era require to be restored to their original specification.

Now fast forward almost half a century to the Scottish Highlands in mid winter. Stalker's son, Steven, aged about twelve, is riding his motorcycle on the single track tarmac road. There is a stretch of ice, then a dry section, followed by another stretch of ice and so it continued.

Steven hit the ice and with a masterly display of balance and throttle control put the bike into a controlled slide. Just before the ice ended he brought the machine upright and hit the dry patch. The throttle was immediately opened and the front wheel airborne in a wheelie. Down again in time to hit the next patch of ice and the process repeated.

"Let me have a go." I asked, wondering if I could still master the technique. Well, I did manage some half-hearted, allright, quarter-hearted slithery slides but wheelies, with those patches of ice ahead? You must be joking!

AUGUST MONDAY, Aug. 7th, 1944 at 2.30 p.m.

MOTOR CYCLE
GRASS TRACK MEETING

Public Recreation Ground, Radcliffe-on-Trent
Nottinghamshire.

Organised by THE EAST MIDLANDS RACING CLUB

Proceeds in aid of —
RADCLIFFE-ON-TRENT
COMFORTS FOR TROOPS FUND

Some of to-day's Officials :
Clerk of the course and Hon Sec. of the meeting... Mr. T. W. TAYLOR
Press Steward ... ... Mr. J. GRAHAM
Gate Steward ... ... Mr. J. S. HODSON
Programme Stewards ... ... Mr. & Mrs. A. RICHMOND
Competitors Steward ... ...Mr. G. SIMMONDS
Pit Marshall ... ... Mr. S. (Ginger) WOOD

Official Programme - - Sixpence

Use of the ground by kind permission of the Parish Council
of Radcliffe-on-Trent.

Further enquiries to
Mr. Pearce, Hon. Sec. E.M.R.C. 116, Loughborough Road, Nottm.

(Above and following page) First grasstrack meeting in the
Midlands since 1939. No petrol so the only way to get there was
by train then push the bikes from the station. Over 40 enthusiasts
managed it, however. Most of the bikes were home tuned
standard machines with overhead camshaft Velocettes the most
popular choice. Only two Speedway J.A.P.'s ridden by Dixon
Spain and A.F.Elliott. A 350cc Grasstrack Special O.K. Supreme
ridden by the brilliant Coventry rider, Ron Carvill. "P. Goodman"
was Peter Goodman of the Goodman family, manufacturers of
Velocette, riding a Velocette loaned by Derby enthusiast, Alf
Briggs. Eric Oliver, riding a borrowed machine, was to become the
World Sidecar Champion.

152

TO-DAY'S ENTRIES

No.	Rider	Machine	Capacity	Town
1	E. D. Stevenson	Velocette	348	Ilkeston
2	D. Bedwell	Ariel	498	East Leake
3	A. R. Ellison	Triumph	350	Birmingham
4	P. Goodman	Vellocette	350	Derby
5	S. Hodson	Vellocette	348	Nottingham
6	G. M. Kay	Vellocette	350	Derby
7	G. Little	Triumph	250	Solihul
9	J. H. Allen	A.C. Special	500	Nottingham
10	G. Morley	Scott	498	Nottingham
11	R. Carvill	O.K Supreme	348	Coventry
12	E. Oliver			Gainsborough
13	A. G. Briggs	Velo. 348, Triumph	498	Derby
14	P. McManns	Vellocette	350	Derby
15	A. A. W. Myers	Vellocette	348	Nottingham
15	S. Pearce	Vellocette	348	Nottingham
17	F. Purslow	Norton	348	Nottingham
18	H Ramskill	Vellocette	348	Stapleford
19	L. Parry	Rudge	499	Salford
20	J. K. Chapman	Indian	500	Manchester
21	G. C. Nantes	Triumph	350	Nottingham
22	T. Gunn	Rudge	500	Rotherham
23	E. Silver	Sunbeam	500	Leicester
24	L Clark	A.C. Special	500	Nottingham
25	D. Spain	Speedway J.A.P.	500	Manchester
26	W. Kent	Douglas	500	Derby
27	J L. Goldingay	A.J.S.	350	Nottingham
28	R. Mason		500	Tamworth
29	E. Robinson	Vellocette	350	Radcliffe-on-Trent
30	S. Heard	A.J.S.	350	Nottingham
30	E. Day	A.J.S.	350	Nottingham
31	J. S. Burnette	A.J.S. 500. Rudge	500	Derby
35	V Fidler	Excelsior	350	Coventry
36	D. J. Ward	Vellocette	350	Coventry
41	L. Tupling	Tupling Special	350	Rotherham
42	J. D. Gibson	Excelsior	248	Dencaster
43	A. F. Elliott	Speedway J.A.P.	500	Leamington Spa

CLASSIFICATION

350 c.c. Class includes all machines not exceeding 350 c.c.

Unlimited Class is open to machines of any capacity.

In the event of both riders who are sharing a machine qualifying for the Final, the rider clocking the best time will be selected.

BOYLE, PRINTER, WEEKDAY CROSS, NOTTINGHAM

(Top) Grasstrack racers at rest! Left to right: believed Norman Carrington, Fron Purslow, Angus Martin, T, me and Jim Staff with his inevitable pipe.
(Middle) They're off ! Ron Carvill leads, as usual, followed by Alf Briggs.
(Bottom) Wheels spinning, Ron Carvill and Dixon Spain make the divots fly as they slide round the final bend, fighting for first place.

Chapter Twenty One
Reg Parnell
and Nephew

Reg Parnell was Derby's most famous racing driver in the immediate pre war and post war period. He came from a large family and Reg was the "baby". His parents kept the Royal Standard pub on Derwent Street, Derby. Reg's elder brother, Bill, started a haulage contracting business and named it "Standard Transport", after the pub. Reg went into the business immediately on leaving school.

Just after the War, Bill's son, Roy, had arranged for one of the firm's lorries to take a contingent of riders and their machines to a Grasstrack Meeting at Grimsby, with us all sharing the cost of the fuel.

We all loaded our machines onto the lorry and sat on the floor for what was probably the most uncomfortable journey of our lives. It was a closed lorry but had a canvas back above the tailboard and this was rolled up to provide us with "ventilation". The problem was that the exhaust fumes were sucked back into the lorry so we breathed these noxious fumes all the way to Grimsby and repeated it on the return run. We ended each journey feeling very sick indeed.

Now for grasstrack racing the 500 Speedway J.A.P. was supreme in the 500cc class but in the 350cc class we all had home tuned and modified machines with "Camshaft Vellers" being the favoured choice. In the late 1930's, however, OK Supreme had produced a 350 purpose built for grasstrack racing. This was the 350 G.T.S. (Grasstrack Special). The engine was a 350 alcohol J.A.P., i.e. the 350 version of the 500 J.A.P. speedway engine. Very few had been made and we regarded them as the ultimate 350 grasstrack machines, only owned by very few riders.

Roy Parnell was one of the fortunate few who owned one of these infinitely desirable 350's. We were all fanatical motorcycle enthusiasts and how we envied him that outstanding 350. We were, however, amazed to be told that he was not particularly interested in motorcycles: He explained that his Uncle Reg was a racing driver and his real interest was racing cars. He was grasstrack racing merely to gain racing experience!

Roy was to go on to race a 1500cc straight eight supercharged Delage engined racing car in 1946 and this is how it came about:
One of the greatest racing car designs of all time was the 1926 1500cc twin cam supercharged straight eight Delage. In the nineteen thirties Dick Seaman had been driving 1500cc ERA's when the great racing car engineer and former works Alfa Romeo driver, Giulio Ramponi, suggested that despite its age, a Delage could beat the 1500cc E.R.A.'s which were the most successful cars in the 1500 class at that time.

The E.R.A. engine was a development of the 1500 six-cylinder, pushrod overhead valve, Riley engine. The great Brooklands motorcycle tuner and T.T. winner of the 1920's, Freddie Dixon, had shown the potential of these engines by fitting six Amal motorcycle carburettors to one of them and had outperformed the Works cars. The first E.R.A.'s in 1934 had 16lbs per square inch boost but the later 1937 models, with Zoller supercharger, had gone up to 28 lbs boost.

A 1500 Delage was obtained and rebuilt by Ramponi with a lightened chassis and Lockheed hydraulic brakes instead of the original mechanical servo system. For such a long obsolete design, then a decade old, to beat the very latest racing cars was probably unmatched in the history of motor racing.

The engine had originally produced 170 bhp at a very modest 7lbs per square inch boost, giving 130mph. Ramponi, however, with very little modification, increased the output to 195bhp. Laurence Pomeroy, the great authority on supercharging and Grand Prix cars, calculated that with an increase to 15lbs boost the engine would have equalled the performance of the post war Alfa Romeo 158.

In 1936, with Dick Seaman at the wheel, it won the R.A.C. 200 mile race in the Isle of Man and at the end of the season, on three consecutive weekends, it won the Coppa Acerbo at Pescara, Italy, the Prix de Berne in Switzerland and the J.C.C. 200 mile race at Brooklands. At the end of that victorious season with the Delage, Dick Seaman was given a place in the Mercedes Grand Prix team.

During the War years one of these incredible engines was on loan to the Rolls Royce Motor Club who intended to use it in a car they were building to race after the War. As far as I know, however, nothing came of this but Reg Parnell built a racing car using one of these engines: Surely the one originally on loan to the Rolls Royce Motor Club?

This is the car that Roy raced impressively in a speed trial at Elstree in 1946 and many people in the motor racing world considered that Roy would have made a very successful racing driver it he had decided to continue with the sport. Although, as far as I know, he did not continue to race he did join his Uncle Reg at Aston Martin when Reg became the racing team manager in the late 1950's.

Reg Parnell's introduction to car racing was the purchase of an unsupercharged two litre Grand Prix Bugatti from the Derby scrapyard of Thomas Hill.......Price £25. His first event was at Donington Park in 1934 but the Bugatti broke its differential while being driven round the paddock! Reg then found that to buy spares for a foreign racing car was going to be prohibitively expensive so the Bugatti was sold.

In 1935, Reg started in earnest. For the 1935 season he bought a very special K2 MG Magnette. The car had a 1086cc supercharged engine and an unique single seater body. It had been owned by Hugh Hamilton who had garaged and maintained it in Italy. In 1934 when winning its class at Pescara it had been timed at an incredible 122mph. Hugh Hamilton had been entered in the Swiss Grand Prix by Whitney Straight in one of the three Maseratis Whitney Straight had bought for the 1934 season, but he was unfortunately killed in the race.

The MG Magnette launched Reg Parnell into motor racing and I understand that Michael McEvoy, of motorcycle fame, had a hand in improving the supercharging. Reg raced the car at Donington, eventually winning a 10 lap handicap event. He continued to race it at Donington in 1936 and, towards the end of the season, started to compete at Brooklands. During the winter of 1936 Reg rebuilt the MG with a new body and a twin-cam cylinder head designed by McEvoy and Pomeroy. In addition, the engine was bored out to 1,400cc.

During 1937 he started in earnest, driving at Donington, Crystal Palace and Brooklands but the season was to end in disaster: Practising for the BRDC "500" Reg went into a slide when high on the banking and his car hit Kay Petre's Works Austin Seven. She was very badly injured and her life was in the balance, though she eventually made a remarkable recovery.

Kay Petre was a petite, feminine, dark haired, very attractive Canadian and "one of the boys" at Brooklands. She had already made her mark at Brooklands in a series of cars including her own two litre Bugatti which she had bought in 1932. She had married Henry Petre, one of the pioneer pilots flying from Brooklands, a man who would have nothing to do with women........until he met Kay!

Reg, however, was not "one of the boys". He was, as they say in the USA, "from the other side of the tracks". In addition he had already gained a reputation as a "Wild man" in a racing car so the result was the suspension of his racing licence. No racing for Reg, then, in 1938, though for the 1939 season, after investigation, his license was restored. For the 1939 season he raced a B.H.W., a much modified five litre Bugatti until War stopped racing.

Also in 1939 Reg decided to build a Grand Prix car which he named the "Challenger". He engaged Allen, the designer, to make the car with an advanced six-cylinder, twin-cam engine and the appearance not unlike the Grand Prix Mercedes. The car was completed in 1939 but, unfortunately, not the engine. This was the car that was raced after the War fitted with the 1500 Delage engine.

Reg had bought Wallfields Farm, Findern near Derby and during the War he bought as many racing cars as he could. Cars belonging to other racing men who were away at the War were also stored at Wallfields Farm and I understand that at one time Reg owned four E.R.A.'s.

Reg's son, Tim, told me that during the War all the E.R.A.'s, other than the Bira cars, were stored at Wallfields Farm and I asked him why they had not kept one or two of the classic racing cars that had gone through their hands. "Well," said Tim "my father thought that if we could keep buying, selling and making a profit, we couldn't be far wrong". So who could argue with that?

After the War Reg was thoroughly immersed in the world of motor racing and his contribution was truly remarkable: For a start his stock of racing cars helped get the sport going again after the War and Formula One owes much to his support of British racing. He drove everything all over Europe and as far afield as New Zealand. He raced the ill fated sixteen cylinder BRM and gained its first race win. He competed in Grand Prix races, the Mille Miglia, The T.T., Le Mans and much more. He raced E.R.A.'s, Maseratis, Works Alfa Romeos, Connaughts, Aston Martins and others.

After retiring from driving in 1957 he managed Aston Martin Racing and after that he managed Yeoman Credit Racing. He even went on to run his own racing team, Reg Parnell Racing. A genius at talent spotting he was instrumental in giving Mike Hailwood, Jim Clarke, John Surtees and others their introduction to racing cars.

Sadly Reg died of a stroke in 1964, aged only 53, but he has left his indelible mark on the world of motor racing.

(Top) 1926 1,500cc straight eight supercharged Grand Prix Delage. Successful in its day then brought back ten years later to challenge the hitherto invincible E.R.A.'s in the hands of Dick Seaman. An achievement unequalled before or since in the world of motor racing.
(Bottom) Late 1930's E.R.A., brilliantly successful in the 1,500cc class in the hands of a number of great drivers including "B. Bira", a Siamese prince.

Chapter Twenty Two
Rolls Royce days

At the end of the War I applied to Rolls Royce for a job on the Technical Staff and was taken on into a very different world from Fletcher's. I worked on aero-engine development in the Test Office at Sinfin, Derby, a far cry from those Dickensian conditions at Fletcher's.

The great pleasure about working at Rolls Royce was the quality of my colleagues. In the Test Office, they were all extremely intelligent men, first class engineers and good guys every one. To work with them was a great privilege: There was so much to learn and they were only too pleased to give you the benefit of their experience. There were many new friends to be made; lots of motorcyclists, too. One of them was Eric Odell. Eric had worked at RR before the War but left to serve in the Army, attaining the rank of Captain but now back to start at the bottom again. Eric was a well educated and thoroughly likeable chap and we quickly became friends. A Scott enthusiast, too.

Another motorcyclist, Vic Fowkes would hammer away, writing reports, in bursts of feverish activity broken by bursting into song! "One meat ball, without the gravy" was one of his favourites. Vic was not only an engineer but a man of many talents: Artist, tap dancer, gifted at amateur dramatics, dance band vocalist and, not least, debonair man-about-town with a wicked moustache!

Vic was a motorcyclist and had a 1927 175cc two-stroke B.S.A. Now this was one of B.S.A.'s most unsuccessful models. When Vic finally bought a motorcar it was an absolutely clapped out Fiat 500 of about 1937 vintage. These were marvellous little cars, real

161

four-cylinder cars in miniature, way ahead of their time and a notable milestone in motoring evolution. Vic's car had about a two-inch layer of whitemetal fragments in the bottom of the sump but despite the almost insuperable problem of obtaining materials, Vic painstakingly rebuilt it to the last nut and bolt.

Vic, in his wisdom, decided that the oil pump was not up to the job so he set to, designed one and made it himself. Not only did it work effectively but after Vic had rebuilt the engine he drove it successfully for 86,000 miles... an incredible mileage for those days. He then sold it, still in running order, for £35.

Among the inspectors was Dick Bray, another top class engineer with a marvellously incisive mind: A big, powerfully built, handsome man.

Glyn Owen came from Holyhead: A first class brain with an abundance of Celtic charm. His brother still lived in Holyhead where he was a professional diver. Not long before I had joined the Test Office he had been working underwater when a heavy piece of machinery slid unexpectedly and immovably trapped his finger. He was faced with two choices: Stay there and drown or cut off his finger. He took out his diver's knife and chose the latter option!

"Jock" Brown was a driver, not an engineer. A diminutive Scotsman with a brilliant, outgoing personality. He managed to obtain all sorts of goods in short supply in the immediate post war world and sold them round the works. He was a natural salesman from whom there was much to learn.

Another denizen of the Test Office was Norman Watkis, an old motorcyclist who had worked at Amac Carburettors in the 1920's. Amac eventually amalgamated with other manufacturers to become Amal Carburettors. It is generally thought that for best results on a motorcycle the inlet and exhaust tracts should be polished and, for racing, there is a lot to be said for it. For touring, however, the inlet tract is better to have an even, shot-blasted effect to give maximum atomisation.

To get this effect in his Amac days they had a simple solution: The cylinder head chosen for treatment would have the inlet tract blanked off with a quantity of steel shot inside. It would then be fastened to a car wheel and driven around. The result would be an even shot-blasted surface. Norman went on to work at McEvoy's so he had a first class background in motorcycles before moving to Rolls Royce.

Norman lived in an isolated house and electricity was provided by his own generator driven by a 250cc Villiers engine. Eventually an overhaul was required but despite all his efforts the flywheel for the flywheel magneto proved immovable. He brought the engine in to work to have another crack at it. Someone had told him that the solution to the problem was "Miracle Oil". Soak it with this magic elixir for 24 hours and the flywheel would have to give. Norman duly dosed it and then went home but Chris Harrison stayed behind and with a powerful extractor and big hammer he removed the reluctant flywheel. He then replaced it but did not tighten it up.

The next morning Norman was persuaded to have another go at removing the flywheel despite his protests that the oil had not been allowed to work for 24 hours. To his absolute amazement the flywheel instantly came off and from then on Norman extolled the virtues of Miracle Oil with evangelical zeal!

Another ex motorcyclist and ex McEvoy employee was Harry Lomas of Milford near Derby. Harry was the father of Bill Lomas who was to become World Motorcycle Champion.

Many Rolls Royce men had a fascinating tale to tell and among them was Horace Leeson. Horace was a friend of Chris Harrison from way back and was a man with an innovative mind. He was the Rolls Royce engineer chosen to accompany Sir Malcolm Campbell on his attempt on the water speed record at Coniston in 1939. The record was taken at 141.74 mph.

The engine in the boat was one of the legendary Rolls Royce "R" (Racing) engines which were an epic milestone in aero engine design. In 1927 Britain won the Schneider Trophy, a seaplane contest held bi-annually. The plane was designed by the immortal R.J. Mitchell who was later to design the Spitfire. The plane was powered by a Napier Lion engine, a marvellous engine, one of which took the Land Speed Record in the "Golden Arrow", driven by John Cobb.

The Napier Lion engine, however, despite its excellence, was now becoming outdated and for the 1929 contest Mitchell appealed to Rolls Royce to design an engine producing 1,500 bhp. At that time the Rolls Royce Kestrel engines, dependent on specification, produced between 500 and 600hp though a scaled up version, the Buzzard, had managed 925bhp. The Buzzard, however, was something of an experiment and at over 36 litres was considered too heavy for fighters. Nonetheless it provided the basis for an engine to contest the Schneider Trophy.

Their aim was 1,500bhp, an enormous task. A complete redesign was started and within three months the new "R" engine was producing 1,545bhp. By the day of the race in August the engine was producing 1,900bhp and the trophy was taken at 357.7mph.

The race was held bi-annually but for 1931, due to the grip of the depression, the government decided that the money could not be found to further develop the engine to produce the extra power now required. Lady Houston, however, stepped forward and guaranteed the £100,000 needed. The engine now produced 2,350 bhp and the Trophy was won for all time. Later in the year, however, it raised the record to 407.5mph.

These incredible engines were used in the Schneider Trophy S6, S6a and S6b seaplanes and for land speed records in Bluebird, Speed of the Wind and Thunderbolt, also for speed records in Miss England II and III and Bluebird II and III. Horace told me that Sir Malcolm Campbell paid a nominal £50 each for the two engines he used in 1939, including enough spares to build a third.

At the time when Lady Houston's £100,000 saved the day she was a seventy four year old, Lambeth born, former actress. Her third husband, Lord Houston, died in 1926 leaving her £6 million, an enormous sum in those days, probably equivalent to about £150 million today. She was a generous benefactor, giving large sums to all sorts of causes from the support of Christianity in Russia to the relief of impoverished Hull Trawlermen.

In 1932, believing that War was imminent, she offered £200,000 for the air defence of London but the Government rejected it saying, in effect, that it was none of her business! Her help in financing the "R" engine, however, provided a fund of knowledge that helped the development of the Merlin and the Griffon engines vital to the winning of World War Two.

My immediate boss was Chris Harrison, just returned from flying Mosquito night fighters through the war torn skies of Occupied Europe and we answered to Ernest Eltis. Ernest had come to England in the late nineteen thirties as a Czechoslovakian refugee. Ernest had an absolutely brilliant mind and it was a pleasure to work for him. A dedicated engineer who eventually became a Rolls Royce Engineering Director.

We all worked on Rolls Royce Griffon development, though some work was still carried out on Merlins. Griffons were big brothers of the Merlins with the same cylinder capacity as the "R" engines but despite an increase of cylinder capacity of over 35% the frontal areas were almost identical: 7.9 square feet compared to 7.5 square feet. The objective of the design was that the Griffon's dimensions should be such that it would be suitable for installation into existing fighters.

Power output was, of course, superior to that of the Merlin and the early examples, with two-speed, single-stage superchargers, produced 1,795bhp at 16,000 feet. The final 101 series with three stage supercharger and Rolls Royce fuel injection produced over 2,000bhp at 20,000 feet. We wrote the reports and analysed the performance of the Griffon engines and it was fascinating work of absorbing interest. A personal success was when I wrote the original test report on the then new Griffon 57, a single stage supercharged engine designed for the Seafire.

My boss, as mentioned, was Chris Harrison and I was fortunate that Chris was a dedicated motorcycle enthusiast who had owned and raced a 1930 Works Norton, once ridden by the great Stanley Woods. Chris, now in his eighties, is still riding and restoring vintage motorcycles. In 1939 Chris decided to buy his first car and was offered the choice of two: A 1929 1500cc "Chain-gang" Frazer Nash or a short chassis Red Label Bentley, price £27.10s each! He chose the Frazer Nash rather than the Bentley with its higher fuel consumption.

Chris was, and continues to be, an engineer to his finger tips. He had worked on Rolls Royce aero-engine testing in the late 1930's and then volunteered for the RAF when the War came. He was sent to America to train as a pilot but his training was interrupted when Rolls Royce requested his transfer to Packards, Detroit, to help them to manufacture Rolls Royce Merlin engines for the war effort. Packards had also produced the huge "Liberty" aero engines in World War One.

When Packards had got Merlin production well under way, Chris went back to flying training in the United States and when this was completed, back to England to fly combat missions. Unlike so many of his colleagues, Chris was fortunate enough to survive despite, on many occasions, embarking on "mission impossible".

Chris was a member of 515 Squadron, flying Mosquitos from Little Snoring, Norfolk. 515 was part of the 100 Group which had been formed to provide fighter escort for the bombers which were hammering Germany. Unfortunately the bombers suffered punishing losses from the German night fighters and the objective of the 100 Group was to attack the these night fighters and their airfields to reduce bomber losses.

On the night of March 30th/31st 1944 there was a 795 bomber raid on Nuremburg but despite the efforts of the 100 group, 95 were lost. Mosquito pilot R.G. "Tim" Woodman actually saw 44 shot down.

During the first World War the German U-boat pens were at Bruges, completely protected from the most powerful bombs of the time by six feet of concrete. In the Second World War the U-boat pens were at La Rochelle on the Atlantic coast of France and it was absolutely essential to do everything possible to stop those deadly sea wolves.

In addition to flying over Germany, Chris flew his share of missions in his Mosquito as a member of the fighter escort to the Lancaster bombers sent to bomb the La Rochelle U-boat pens. They had to cross the Cherbourg Peninsular, run the gauntlet of deadly anti-aircraft fire, drop their bombs at La Rochelle, then back to run the gauntlet again. Many planes were lost and many brave men died but none of them had the slightest chance of even chipping the paint off a U-boat because the huge thickness of concrete, which was, I believe, eighteen feet thick, made them completely invulnerable.

Chris could, and should, write a book about his wartime experiences but one does spring instantly to mind: When 515 Squadron arrived at Little Snoring airfield, the personnel were housed in huts. In Chris's hut, the pilot in bed number three only flew two missions before being shot down. A replacement pilot arrived and was given bed number three. A few days later he, also, failed to return. The next pilot arrived and he, too, only lasted a few days. No pilot from bed number three ever completed three missions.

Now it goes without saying that young men of those days were not superstitious: As Doctor Johnson said about the belief in ghosts a couple of centuries ago "All argument is against it but all feeling is for it." But superstitious or not, no other pilot chose to sleep in bed number three.

I could not have wished for a better boss than Chris who was endlessly helpful and only too happy to hand on to me his enormous store of knowledge. Much as I enjoyed my work in the Test Office there were many opportunities to sell motorcycles during working hours which I found impossible to resist! Chris would turn a blind eye if work was not too badly affected but if he felt that it was, then reprimands could not be avoided!

When Chris did reprimand me it was always justified and it was done politely, firmly and without rancour. The very model, in fact, of how it should be done. In consequence there was never any sense of injustice and no harm was done to our relationship. In later years, as an employer in a similar situation I always tried, not always with success, to follow Chris' example. When the time came to leave Rolls Royce and start out in business it was a wrench to leave such a rewarding job and such marvellous fellow workers.

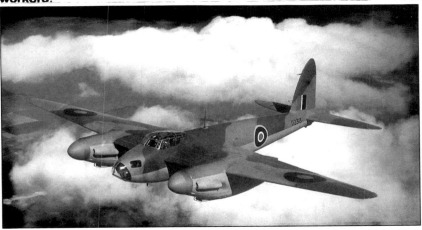

The Mosquito, famous "Wooden Wonder", powered by twin Merlin engines. Chris Harrison flew them many times on "mission impossible" over occupied Europe. His favourite, "Katie", now sleeps at the bottom of the North Sea.

167

(Top) Two of the leading Nottingham enthusiasts, both marvellous characters. Left: Fron Purslow. Right: A.A.W. Bill Myers.
(Middle) Angus "Intl the bend" Martin on a much modified 500 Manx Norton. No, "intl" is not a misprint: it's Northern Irish for "into"!
(Bottom) Fred Tuck, professional Speedway rider on his 500 Excelsior-J.A.P.. I bought a new Speedway J.A.P. engine from him to fit into my Speedway J.A.P..

Chapter Twenty Three
Peace at Last

The War was over at last: Now it had to be paid for! Before the War Britain had huge overseas earnings from investments overseas but when the War started, dollars were needed to pay for essential war material and, not least, petrol from America. Petrol during the war came from America, as petrol from the Middle East is a post war development.

At first dollars were used to pay for war supplies but when these were spent, America suggested that dollar shares and securities held in Britain were handed over as payment. British citizens holding such shares handed them to the Government and were paid in sterling. When the War ended, however, the interest, that would have been paid in dollars and would have been an enormous help in reducing our balance of payments problem, was lost.

When those dollar securities, too, were exhausted, the next step was "Lend-Lease": America would continue to supply the desperately needed supplies without payment on the understanding that they would be paid for after the War. This was to be the sting in the tail!

Forgive me if I now divert for a moment.

The time is the 1930's, the hey-day of Hollywood. The executives of one of the great studios are at a meeting to decide what the subject of the next film should be. Chief Executive, Stan Goldfinn, paces the floor, chomping on a cigar with delusions of grandeur: It thinks it's a marrow!

He asks for suggestions but when they are offered......Romance, Drama, Foreign Intrigue, Horror.... they are all dismissed with an impatient wave of his cigar.

Finally he stops abruptly, stabs the air triumphantly with his marrow, sorry, cigar and shouts "Goddit, Guys. Let's make a Western. *Why do I have to think of everything?*"

The scene now changes to Number Ten Downing Street in the post war period. The Prime Minister....any Prime Minister....has called a Cabinet meeting. With everyone seated he addresses the Cabinet: "The economic situation that we face, gentlemen, is grave and worsens by the hour. Despite our planned changes of policy and unfortunately unplanned U-turns, nothing has succeeded. Have you any suggestions on how we can avert the coming crisis?"

The room falls silent. Shoes surreptitiously shuffle on the floor under the Cabinet table. Pencils are pensively chewed, but no suggestions are forthcoming.

Finally the Prime Minister speaks: "Gentlemen, the situation in which we find ourselves leaves no alternative: We will devalue the pound. *Why do I have to think of everything?*"

Fiction? Of course! But could there be a grain of truth in it?

To we tiny toilers out there at the sharp end, trying to earn a living, it appeared that in the post war world British politicians regarded devaluation's as an all too easy option as the Country staggered from one dollar crisis to the next.

The first of these devaluations came in the early post war years, announced by the ascetic Stafford Cripps and there were no holds barred: He devalued the pound by a massive 29%. Harold Wilson, at a later date, was to add, or should I say deduct, his two pennorth by further devaluing the pound by another 14% adding his never-to-be-forgotten assurance that it did not mean that the pound in your pocket had been devalued!

In addition there were insidious devaluations when policies were adopted that would have the effect of devaluing the pound without the embarrassment of having to make a public announcement.

When politicians had no choice but to defend devaluation they always presented it as *a good thing*! Rather like telling a man who had lost both legs how lucky he was because of the amount he would save on shoe leather!

(Top) One of the all time greats: 1938 Triumph Tiger 80. They went like a bomb and responded to tuning, too. I rode mine on the road, over the Clwyian Range, in trials, scrambles and even on grasstracks.

(Bottom) 150cc ohv Triumph. Only made for 1933/4 but in my opinion one of the prettiest lightweights of its day. Performance was restricted by the 65/70 octane petrol of the time but, even so, great fun to ride. The 150 O.H. valvers of that era pointed the way in which design was going.

(Top) Brother Brian was never a motorcyclist so I do not have a photograph of him on a motorcycle. Next best is a photograph of him with a friendly arm around the lovely Jean Rose, (does that arm look a little TOO friendly?). She is sitting on my 1934 350cc overhead camshaft Velocette.

(Bottom) T and I in an unusual pose! 350 WD Matchless on the right, 1938 350cc A.J.S. on the left.

172

Chapter Twenty Four
The Burdens of Peace

The end of the war in Europe came in May 1945 though just before the end the Germans, against all the odds, mounted a furious offensive. They had done the same thing in 1918 but, once again, it was doomed to failure.

Despite devastating bombing the Japanese carried on with the War until finally the atom bombs on Hiroshima and Nagasaki later in 1945 finally ended the War.

War weary Britain looked forward to shaking off the shackles of wartime restrictions and shortages to get on with the brave new world. At last a new era had dawned and basic petrol was restored in June 1945.

Although the British people held Winston Churchill in the highest regard as the architect of victory they did NOT have similar feelings about his Party. The Conservative Party had been in power for most of the 1930's and no-one wanted to return to a repeat of those depression ridden years. The Conservatives had missed their opportunity in the 1930's, so the reasoning went, now was the time for a change.

The new Labour government was elected by a landslide victory immediately after the war and their promise of an entirely new world with its extensive programme of nationalisation, fair shares for all, extensive social reforms and a new health service were entirely in tune with the mood of the times.

So although the nation was exhausted and faced massive dollar debts to pay for the War, it was still a Great Power. or so we all thought. We all stood to attention when "God Save The King" was played at the end of cinema performances. The War had been won and the British Empire had been made safe from what Winston Churchill called "The Nazi hordes".

What none of us, the public, realised was that the Empire, of which we had been so proud, far from being saved by the War was inevitably headed for disintegration. The crushing post war burdens the nation had to bear made it impossible for it to sustain the role of a World Power.

On a happier note, the first step towards the new Utopia was made on New Year's Day 1947 when, heralding the first of the great nationalisation steps, the Coal Industry was nationalised. No longer would the exploited miners be at the mercy of the rapacious mine owners. All collieries had on their notice boards on January the first 1947 the following message "This colliery is now managed by the National Coal Board on behalf of the people."

So now the miners, as members of the public, owned their pits and strikes would now be a thing of the past, wouldn't they? Wouldn't they?

No they wouldn't! The South Yorkshire miners soon walked out on strike to continue their unbroken tradition!

In early 1947 the country was hit by a bitterly cold spell; coal production dropped and heavy snow hindered transport from the pit heads. Lack of coal brought power cuts which slowed and even stopped factories, shooting unemployment up from half a million to two million.

House building came to a standstill. Thousands squatted in empty buildings and as the Brave New World appeared to be going into reverse thousands emigrated and there were queues outside Australia House applying for the £10 assisted passage.

The bitter winter was followed by floods and half a million acres of wheat were ruined. Rationing, far from ending, was worse than during the War. The meat ration was little enough but it was cut twice during 1947 and bread was rationed for the first time. In November even potatoes were rationed, also for the first time. The petrol ration was withdrawn, effectively bringing our embryo motorcycle business to a standstill and very nearly destroying it, but I will return to this later. "Spivs", cashing in on shortages, sold goods in short supply at inflated prices.

So was it all bad? Surprisingly, no. It was, with hindsight, considered to be the healthiest diet the British public had ever "enjoyed". To divert for a moment, back in 1901, of the 12,000 young Manchester men who wanted to join the Army, only 10% were fully fit and the majority had teeth so rotten that they could not chew properly. Today, of course, as far as food is concerned, we suffer from an "embarras des richesses".

Television was back after having closed down in 1939 but as this only applied to the London area this had no effect on us. Even so, it was a start.

The "New Look" arrived with dramatically long skirts after the short skirts of wartime though the government urged the necessity to retain short skirts to save cloth.

Princess Elizabeth and Lieutenant Philip Mountbatten married in November and this was a bright spot in the news.

National Service was brought in so eighteen year olds had to join the Services or go down the pits as "Bevin Boys": An unexpected move with the War behind us.

The British people had accepted all the privations of war and the continuing privations of the post war world with unfailing stoicism but social changes were inevitable. Many hasty wartime marriages could not endure and there were 60,000 divorces in 1947 which, although a fraction of today's rate, was still ten times the pre war figure.

Although the Country had more than enough problems of its own there were still wider responsibilities: 400,000 tons of wheat had to be sent to help to feed former enemies so we had to accept bread rationing. 15,000 British were helping to administer the British Zone in Germany. British troops were also attempting to keep the peace between Jews and Palestinians, but with conspicuous lack of success!

Lord Louis Mountbatten was appointed Viceroy of India but India was in turmoil. Hindus and Moslems desperately wanted the British out but had little idea of what to do when it happened.

Later in the year independence was granted and to most of us it came as a complete shock, out of the blue. The huge sub-continent was split into India and Pakistan. Once the British were out the Muslims and the Hindus slaughtered each other. The

Muslims would send trainloads of thousands of corpses to the Hindus and the Muslims would do the same back.

On a personal note, we gained another family member in 1945. Having brought up two boys, my mother adopted a little girl, Susan.

Susan was a most welcome addition to our family and we were all delighted to welcome her.

(Top) A racing Douglas of the late 1920's hauled out of none too honourable retirement to snarl in anger one more time.
(Bottom) Now you've seen everything........ a Speedway B.S.A.! But remember you saw it here first! Just look at that monstrous knee hook: Speedway style gone over the top! B.S.A.'s did, indeed, dabble briefly with Speedway but I would have thought that this was a standard B.S.A. of the early thirties modified for grasstrack racing. Unless, of course, you know different!

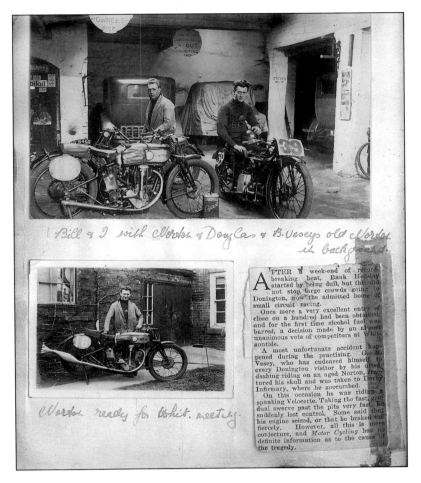

Bill & I with Norton & Douglas & B. Vesey's old Norton in background.

Norton ready for Whit. meeting.

AFTER a week-end of record-breaking heat, Bank Holiday started by being dull, but this did not stop large crowds going to Donington, now the admitted home of small circuit racing.

Once more a very excellent entry of close on a hundred had been obtained, and for the first time alcohol fuel was barred, a decision made by an almost unanimous vote of competitors at Whitsuntide.

A most unfortunate accident happened during the practising. G. R. Vesey, who has endeared himself to every Donington visitor by his ultra dashing riding on an aged Norton, fractured his skull and was taken to Derby Infirmary, where he succumbed.

On this occasion he was riding a spanking Velocette. Taking the fast, cruel, dual swerve past the pits very fast, he suddenly lost control. Some said that his engine seized, or that he braked too fiercely. However, all this is mere conjecture, and *Motor Cycling* has no definite information as to the cause of the tragedy.

Local enthusiast Joe Hoult at Wall's Garage, Melbourne. He is sitting on his late 1920's racing Douglas. In the foreground is the 1930 Ex-Works 500 Norton he rode in the 1934 Manx Grand Prix and later sold to Chris Harrison. The machine behind is Bob Vesey's 1927 500 ohv Norton, tuned by Bob Vesey and Frank Platt of Belper. This bike really flew and was considered to be the equal in performance of the 1930 Ex-Works Norton. The sign at the back reads "The man who lends the tools is out collecting them".

177

(Top) 1947 Triumph Tiger 100. One of the most desirable
machines of its day. Similar to the 1939 model but now with
Triumph telescopic front forks.
(Bottom) B.S.A. B33 500cc, Very similar to the B31 350cc. Basic
engine design late 1930's but now with B.S.A. telescopic forks.
Well made B.S.A. value.

Chapter Twenty Five
The Motorcycle Scene

Although T and I had long decided to start out in the motorcycle business after the War there was no question of immediately starting up as the "Direction of Labour" order meant that you could not leave your job without official consent.

But grass track racing had started in a limited way at Radcliffe on Trent in August 1944 and this was to continue and expand in the post war period. Petrol was back so we were on the road again and able to buy and sell. I had moved to Rolls Royce at the end of the War and T had always worked there.

The period from the end of the War to leaving Rolls Royce and starting out in business in 1947 was a time of hectic activity for us. Bikes bought and sold, premises found and refurbished, all preparations made to be ready to start on our own as soon as it became possible.

Servicemen returning from the war meant a huge demand for motorcycles and all those machines laid up during the War had to be hauled out from lock up garages and garden sheds for reconditioning. The demand had to be met by second-hand machines though a few new machines started to trickle through from 1946. The first post War B.S.A.'s arrived at Ingles at the Cavendish Derby: They were the B.S.A. agents and the bikes were M.20 500cc side-valve models as supplied to the Army during the war but now in black with silver painted tanks.

Ex-War Department (Ex-WD) machines were also coming onto the market in considerable numbers: 350 Matchlesses with both telescopic and girder forks, 500 16H side-valve Nortons and

B.S.A. M20's, 350 Ariels and even a few 350 Triumphs and 350 MAF Velocettes. We bought and sold all these models.

The American forces had used 500 vee-twin Indians and 750 vee-twin Harley Davidsons and although we sold them, too, we regarded them as clumsy brutes which handled like a double decker bus, suitable only for sidecar haulage. Their hopeless handling, woolly vee-twin side-valve engines, ridiculous hand gearchange and foot clutches condemned them to nothing else.

Mosquito aircraft had used torpedo shaped "Drop tanks" to increase their fuel load and hence range over occupied Europe. They were cast adrift or "Dropped" when their fuel load was used up. They were just the right size and shape for a motorcycle sidecar body and many were snapped up by the big motorcycle dealers like Pride and Clark and sold at modest prices for motorcyclists to convert into sidecar bodies. Many of them were fitted to those Ex.WD Indians, Harleys, M.20 B.S.A.'s and 16H Nortons.   The War in Europe had ended in May 1945 and a petrol ration was restored in June. Despite all the vicissitudes the feel-good factor had arrived for we motorcyclists, though the phrase itself had yet to be invented. Only two or three gallons a month but used with care it would go a long way. One hundred miles to the gallon was achievable from many machines if ridden at modest speeds.

In the world of motorcycling there were exciting developments: There had already been news of the post war Triumph range, basically 1939 twins, though now with the new Triumph telescopic fork. There were whispers about the new 1,000cc Vincent range and, in addition, there was leaked news of the brand new B.S.A. 500 twin.

The proposed 350 Douglas twins were entirely new with engines across the frame like B.M.W.'s and with exciting front and rear suspension. For most makes, however, rear suspension was in the future.

Some famous names were never to appear again after the War, for example New Imperial, Rudge, Levis, Coventry Eagle and O.K.Supreme, but the manufacturers who had kept in production during the War making motorcycles were soon to change from khaki to black for the civilian market, though most of their production was earmarked for export.

Prices were considered to be dreadfully high and boosted even higher by one-third purchase tax. Prices were, of course, very high compared to 1939 because of inflation. Purchase tax was a dreadful burden and the rate was to see-saw about in the post war stop-go economy. It had been introduced in 1940 and for a long time many people thought it was only a temporary measure but this optimism was unfortunately misplaced. The Government loved to raise and lower the rate to stimulate or put brakes on the economy as they saw fit. It was never to be abolished until finally replaced by VAT.

Millions of dollars were still needed to pay for the War and "Export or die" was the slogan of the day so most motorcycles had to be sold abroad to earn those precious dollars. The country was facing economic bankruptcy, the shortage of materials was acute, wartime controls were still in force and the direction of labour meant that no-one could leave their job without Government consent.

To buy a new motorcycle in 1945 the buyer had to show an essential need and had to obtain a Government "License to acquire".

So manufacturers kept change to a minimum other than the provision of telescopic forks, pioneered by Matchless during the War with their remarkable "Teledraulic" fork.

Pre war second-hand machines were the mainstay of the market followed by huge numbers of Ex-WD machines. Spares were a problem and tyres, when you could get them, were made of synthetic rubber that wore out rapidly, though there was no truth in the rumour that they were made of compressed monkey nut shells!

The Triumph 500 vertical twin of 1937 was to change the design of motorcycle engines throughout the world. All other major manufacturers had no choice but to follow suit. The leading British manufacturers all had 500 vertical twins on the drawing board and most were to have them ready for sale by the end of the 1940's.

In September 1946 the B.S.A. 500cc vertical twin was announced with a well designed duplex frame. It was, however, without rear suspension and it was not until 1949 that plunger rear suspension was available.

A photograph of the Ariel 500 vertical twin appeared in the motorcycle press in 1946 but it did not come onto the market until 1948.

Electrics on most larger machines were provided by a Lucas magneto and dynamo or both combined as a magdynamo. Towards the end of the 1940's plunger rear suspension was available from most manufacturers though Triumph introduced their spring hub as early as 1947. It is fashionable to dismiss it today because of its limited movement but at the time it was a real improvement.

Most machines from 350 upwards had four speed positive stop gearboxes as in 1939 and B.S.A.'s made handy little 250's in O.H.V. and side-valve form with three speed positive stop gearboxes. There were many basic models up to 200cc with Villiers engines. Triumph were the first to announce their post war range with their 500cc twins with their own telescopic fork. A.J.S. and Matchless quickly followed. Single cylinder 350 and 500 models with, of course, their wartime designed "Teledraulic" forks.

In August B.S.A. announced a brand new design with the B.S.A. telescopic fork. The engine was a development of the excellent Val Page 350 and 500 single cylinder models designed in the late 1930's. This machine was the B31, later to be followed by the 500 B33 and the trials versions, B32 and B33.

In 1929 there were three quarters of a million motorcycles and combinations on the British roads but then came the depression! This cut numbers down, year by year, so that by 1939 there were only about 400,000 bikes on the road. By mid 1946, however, there were to be half a million machines on the road.

In early 1946 B.S.A. announced the revolutionary Sunbeam S7. This was a 500cc vertical twin but the engine was in line i.e. one cylinder behind the other whereas most vertical twins had their cylinders side by side. It was an all alloy overhead camshaft engine with car type unit construction gearbox and four speed foot change. It was shaft drive, plunger rear suspension and sported huge sixteen inch balloon tyres.

Revolutionary it might have been but motorcyclists are notoriously conservative when it comes to actually handing over their hard earned brass, as distinct from merely dreaming!

Chapter Twenty Six
The BSA Combination

With basic petrol back many opportunities had opened up. With bikes to transport, T and I bought a 1927 770cc B.S.A. and sidecar from Joe Hoult of Melbourne. Joe had ridden in the 1934 Manx Grand Prix on the 500 Ex Works Norton that he had later sold to Chris Harrison.

We removed the sidecar and fitted a flat wooden platform with a post at each end. A motorcycle could be put on the platform and tied at each post and at a pinch you could put one either side.

The outfit had been standing in a damp garage throughout the War and quite a lot of work had to be done. 1927 was the first year that this model had drum brakes all round and all wheels, even the sidecar, were interchangeable. Tyres were useless, of course, so remoulds were bought from the Homerton Rubber Co., who advertised in The Motor Cycle, price twenty five shillings each.

The interior of the tank was badly rusted so we cleaned it with Hydrochloric acid. The engine had to be rebuilt and the big end was fitted with new rollers made by T's dad in Rolls Royce Toolroom. Unfortunately they proved to be a failure and were replaced by a good second hand big end assembly from Gaggs of Alfreton Road, Nottingham.

Gaggs were major suppliers of second hand motorcycle spares for decades and were famous for their illiterate adverts in the motorcycle press. Their slogan was "Tie the label on that damaged part and send it to Gaggs".

Their shop was a delight, crammed with second hand spares of all kinds. Old sweet tins were packed with spares: the tins bore the slogan "I Like Broncho Berries." Don't ask me what Broncho

Berries were because I have never eaten one or seen any for sale anywhere!

Having broken up hundreds or, more probably, thousands of motorcycles during his lifetime, Mr. Gagg Senior used to say towards the end of his career "I've put my hammer through a fortune!"

The B.S.A. had a hand pump in the oil compartment in the petrol tank and also a mechanical pump. B.S.A. were not placing too much reliance on these new fangled mechanical pumps and had retained the traditional oil pump as a belt and braces safety measure: Just as well because the mechanical pump on this engine never worked so we had to rely on the hand pump. We gave a shot of oil about every five miles and amazing though it may seem, this system worked perfectly well and we never seized the engine.

We rushed on to get the B.S.A. completed in time to drive over to Rhyl for a long weekend in February 1946 and finally the great day arrived: The bike was ready to go...well, almost!

For local trips on the B.S.A. combination a passenger would sit on the flat wooden platform and rest his back against the rear post but for the Rhyl run we had bolted down a car rear seat with the matching backrest fastened to the rear post. There was, of course, no protection from the weather: An omission we were to regret!

We had planned an early start but unavoidable last minute work on the outfit delayed us so we were unable to get away until afternoon. On our way at last with the rebuilt engine running very well but when darkness came the ancient dynamo decided to give up. We got as far as Nantwich then pulled into the station forecourt to attempt to carry out repairs.

T was always excellent with electrics and we struggled away getting colder and colder but without success. Suddenly we had a brilliant idea: Push the outfit into the station waiting room where we would be warm and have better light in which to work.

There was a roaring fire and the only other occupants were a courting couple canoodling in the corner; they took no notice of us nor we of them!

During the journey the petrol tank had started to leak and this meant petrol leaking onto the wooden floor of the station waiting room...not a good idea with a blazing fire! But another brainwave...

why not use the mat outside to soak up the petrol? In came the mat with, believe it or not, WELCOME imprinted on it.

Finally we thought we had solved the problem so the outfit was wheeled out and started up but no result. We then revved the engine and the dynamo cut in enthusiastically and blew all the bulbs: It then relapsed into sulky inactivity!

Still getting nowhere and short of suitable spanners we decided to seek help so off we went to the local cycle shop in the main street. It was closed, of course, but we went round the back and the friendly proprietor allowed us to use his work bench. We had removed the dynamo and started work on it.

It was a huge, untidy workshop and he kindly lent us the tools and soldering equipment we needed. He and his family lived at the shop and at the other end of the workshop was a table where the proprietor and his family sat eating their evening meal. Such a scene would be unthinkable today: There we were working away at one end of the workshop while the family were happily eating their dinner at the other.

Still no luck with the dynamo, then we had yet another brilliant idea! A flash of inspiration rather like that which hit Archimedes in his bath when he realised that a floating object displaces its own weight in water and he leaped out shouting "Eureka".

Definitely an eureka moment for us, however, and the instant solution? Cycle lamps! Three cycle lamps instantly purchased from our helpful cycle dealer and some red paper found to convert one into a rear lamp. All three fastened into position and with thanks to our benefactor we were on our way like schoolboys released for their holidays.

This time all was well: No further hold-ups and we drove merrily through the night. Although both rider and passenger were equally exposed to the elements it was, for some reason, much colder in, or should I say on, the sidecar.

The last leg of the journey was on the "bottom" road through Flint and Mostyn. On this stretch a young airman flagged us down for a lift. He was on leave, attempting to get to his home in Rhyl, so he joined me on the sidecar.

Bitterly cold but in excellent spirits we hurtled through the night, singing away. Rhyl at last in the early hours of the morning after an epic ride that had taken just over ten hours for the one hundred and five miles.

Great to be in Stella Maris again so the mixture as before: A marvellous time was had by all before we had to sadly leave it all behind and head back to Derby.

Only just out of Rhyl on the road to Prestatyn the headwind was so strong that the B.S.A.'s clutch slipped badly and we hardly made headway. We turned round to go back only to find that the clutch was now biting well enough, so round again for another try.

This time we managed somehow and on we went. We hadn't been going long, however, when it started to snow and the snow got worse and worse! We quickly resembled two snowmen but we struggled on, getting colder and colder!

Chester, Tarporley and Nantwich behind us, then just beyond Pipegate we stopped at a farm and asked if they would be kind enough to let us have a bag of straw and they gladly did so. I was in the sidecar and I put my legs in the sack to get some protection from the elements. The wind, however, whistled through the straw and I was little better off.

Just beyond the Market Drayton turnoff the road to Stone was signposted as blocked so we had to fork left for Trentham, a long way round. Dark by now, of course and the snowstorm was getting even worse. Our cycle lamps wouldn't have been much use even it they had not been covered in snow!

Trentham at last then the long run through all those little villages towards Uttoxeter. No other vehicles on the road and at the foot of every hill lorries had been abandoned, unable to get a grip on the snowbound road. With our lighter combination, however, we were able to keep going.

At Tean we saw the lights of a huge dairy and pulled in, frozen stiff. A number of stranded lorry drivers there and having regained some semblance of warmth we decided to sleep in the boiler house. Sleep, however, was impossible so we decided to hit the road again.

Back on the road with visibility down to a few yards the throttle started to stick open. After stopping to free it a few times we realised that the snow sucked into the carburettor intake was freezing the throttle slide into position, so what to do? Again a flash of inspiration: Simply hold the throttle half open then *let* the slide freeze up and control the speed by use of the ignition lever.

This makeshift solution worked well enough so the two mobile snowmen struggled on for that last twenty miles.

Back to 128 Stonehill Road, Derby at last in the early hours of the morning having beaten the record time for the outward journey: This time it took over eleven hours!

On the radio next morning it announced "All roads in Derbyshire are impassable". Not true: We had made it!

Epic rides to Rhyl on every kind of motorcycle and in every kind of weather were to remain a feature of those years but this was one of the toughest!

The B.S.A. was to prove an excellent workhorse, transporting all kinds of loads: Sand, cement, bricks, steel girders, rubble and, of course, people and motorcycles. On snow covered roads in Derby we would see a bus queue then lock the handlebars hard over. The outfit would then go into a sideways slide, apparently out of control. The bus queue would scatter, screaming in anguish, certain that their last hour had come. Just before the bike was due to hit the kerb, however, we would straighten up the handlebars and the bike would sail along perfectly under control as it had been all along. Very reprehensible, I know, something you, personally, would never dream of doing...but great fun!

THE PATHFINDERS' MOTOR CYCLE CLUB

(Affiliated to the A.C.U.)

PALIN TROPHY TRIAL

SUNDAY, 7th OCTOBER, 1945

Start, 11.30 a.m.   "The Greyhound" Hotel, Cromford

Average Speed, 20 m.p.h.

ROUTE.	Section No.	Miles.	First Man's Time.
L ; S.O. over main road ; **R** after river bridge ; **S.O.** ; **L** in village ; bear **L** at X roads ; **L** to **HIGH LEAS SPLASH (Observed)**	1	3	11·39
R ; S.O. up hill ; **L** to **DETHICK LANE (Observed)**	2	3·5	11·40½
S.O. at ~~d~~ ; **S.O.** over road (DANGEROUS) ; **L** and immediately **R ; S.O. ; R** at X lanes ; **L** at T roads ; **R** at main road ; **S.O.** X roads, down steep hill past Lord Nelson Inn ; **S.O.** along main road ; **L (S.P.** Holymoorside) ; **L** at T roads ; **L ; L** at X roads in village ; **S.O. ; S.O. ; L** to **HUNGER HILL (Observed)**	3	13	12·09
R at road ; first **L ; S.O.** X roads ; **S.O. ; L ; R** hairpin to **ROB RIDDING (Observed)**	4	15·5	12·16½
S.O. up hill ; first **R ; S.O.** X roads ; **S.O. ; L** at main road ; at bottom of steep hill sharp **L** to **SYDNOPE (Observed, 3 sections)**	5 6 7	19	12·27
R at top ; **R** hairpin at cottage ; **L** at bottom of hill (CAUTION— other competitors in opposite direction) ; **L** at main road ; bear **L** at **S.P.** Matlock ; **L** at main road ; first **R (S.P.** Winster) ; **L** at X roads ; **R** in village ; **L ; S.O.** to **BIRCHOVER (Observed, 2 sections)**	8 9	22·5	12·37½
R at top ; **L** hairpin ; **L** at T roads (hairpin) ; **L** at main road ; first **R** at mirror ; up hill ; **R** to "Miner's Standard" **CHECK**	—	25·5	12·46½

(Top) Wonderful, challenging days over magnificent Derbyshire Trials country.

Chapter Twenty Seven
Mud, Mud, Glorious Mud

Derbyshire is a lovely county situated in the centre of England. It starts south of Burton-on-Trent and extends north of Sheffield. The variety of scenery varies from the rich farmland in the south to the mountains and moorland in the north. Derbyshire, in fact, has everything but the sea.

In motorcycling terms the north of the county provides a marvellous selection of trials sections, many of them with memorable names.

All these trials sections provide a wide variety of different challenges and we motorcyclists in Derby were very fortunate in having them on our doorstep. We all tried our hand at trials riding and thoroughly enjoyed ourselves.

We were, of course, riding bikes of the 1930's and the difference between a standard machine and a trials model was not very much. 350cc machines were a favoured choice but 250's and 500's were also used. The advantage of a 250 was light weight, of great benefit when lugging the bike over the boulder strewn surface of Hollinsclough. The 500's had the advantage of extra power but, again, offset by the disadvantage of more weight.

Bikes of the era had rigid rear ends, i.e. no rear suspension so a four inch rear tyre was fitted, run at only a few pounds per square inch to provide maximum grip. Instead of a nineteen inch front wheel a twenty-one inch rim was fitted with a narrow tyre, usually three inch compared to the normal 3.25". This gave us extra ground clearance. An upswept exhaust system and a one eighth of an inch thick steel undershield protected the crankcase from boulders.

That was it, as far as we were concerned, though if sold new as a trials machine, wide ratio gears were also supplied. This meant a low bottom and second gear with a wide gap to normal third and top. We would lower all ratios by fitting a larger rear wheel sprocket. With this work completed we were ready to go!

The start to a trial would often be held at the unusually named "Bull 'i Thorn" Inn on the Ashbourne to Buxton Road, right in the middle of superlative trials country and a variety of functional, and dysfunctional machines would congregate to tackle the Derbyshire trials sections: High Leas Splash, Hunger Hill, Hognaston Dumble, a lovely name, Flash Bottom a " remarkable" one, Rob Ridding, Slaley Moor, Birchover and not least, Sydenope (say it slowly).* There are many others, of course, not forgetting the fearsome Hollinsclough on the Derbyshire/Staffordshire border.

Marvellous, challenging days in beautiful country followed by the ride back to Derby, tired but happy.

Norman Watkiss telling me about his trials riding days a generation before us, having spent the day riding over the same trials country and ending up at Derby, would go with his friends to Derby's Palais de Danse and, still in their riding gear, would shout from the balcony to the girls below, "Hotcha, baby", a ritual mating call almost incomprehensible to later generations!

In the flatter counties of England trials sections had to rely on mud to provide a challenge to riders. In Derbyshire, however, we have the tremendous advantage of real trials country with hills and hazards galore.

Steep, uphill boulder strewn gullies offer a formidable challenge in dry weather but in wet weather with the boulders coated with slippery mud they are almost impossible to surmount "clean" i.e. without putting a foot down or, worse, "paddling" the bike along the worst bits!

It is the task of the trials organiser to make these sections almost impossible and the rider faces the challenge of tackling these greasy boulders and teeth jarring rock steps without the rear wheel spinning helplessly and losing all grip. The art is a combination of balance and the delicate touch of the throttle hand: Too much throttle and the wheel spins, too little and you stall, so the throttle has to be constantly altered to "feel" the machine over the terrain.

One day trials are not races against the clock and the distance covered in a day is probably in the order of eighty to one hundred miles. So you ride from, say, High Leas Splash to Dethick Lane and the observers check the points lost on that section. Then on to the next section, say Hunger Hill when the process is repeated.

The beauty of these events run by local motorcycle clubs is that the ordinary motorcycle club member can " have a go". He may not come near the top but he has all the enjoyment of competing and riding those magnificent trials sections.

A grass track circuit is usually an oval on a flat grass surface and, like speedway, it is ridden anti-clockwise   A scramble is a cross between grass track racing and a trial. It is a race against the clock over varied terrain... hills, rocks, mud...the lot! Challenging, exhilarating riding.

So the ordinary motorcycle club member had the opportunity to ride in trials, grass tracks and trials with a more or less standard machine, though the 500 Speedway J.A.P. models eventually dominated the 500cc class in grass track racing.

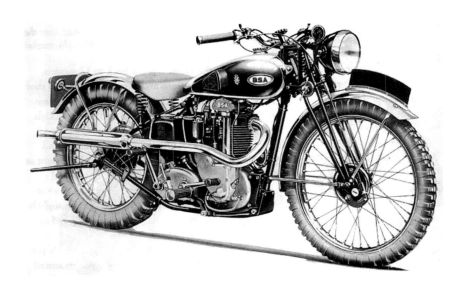

Mid 1930's 350cc Trials B.S.A.

(Top) Years of work ahead. Work started to convert the old stables at 25 Melbourne Street Derby to "The finest motorcycle workshop in Derby". All that rubble had to be transported by our 1927 770cc B.S.A. vee-twin with a packing case bolted to the sidecar platform.

(Bottom) We made the first and third windows. Large middle window bought as scrap from Thomas Hill scrapyard at ten bob (50p) a hundredweight. They are still in place.

Chapter Twenty Eight
Business Premises Acquired

To start in business we needed workshop premises and in that post war world with so many businesses getting started, premises were hard to find and what few were available were quickly snapped up. Finally, in 1945, we were fortunate enough to discover 25 Melbourne Street: Old stables two storeys high, 40 ft. long by 15 ft. wide with its adjoining yard 40 ft. by 20 ft. Just what we needed.

A young chap named Maurice Riley had made a start in the motor trade there with his pal, Peter Le Vack. He had called the place Maurice Riley Garages, though they were never there full-time. Peter was a motorcycle enthusiast, having persuaded a 1920's "Big port" A.J.S. to travel at phenomenal speeds and written to the motorcycle press about it.

We had to buy their welding tackle and other equipment but it was not expensive and we were then allowed to take over their weekly tenancy at £1 a week. The owner was a Miss Currie, an elderly spinster who lived in a large, forbidding Victorian house at the bottom of nearby Leopold Street with decor that appeared to be unchanged from before World War One.

Melbourne Street is in a very convenient location, not far from the town centre. It is a street of Coronation Street type terraced houses but No. 25 is behind them, reached via an opening just over the width of a car. The higher story has two shuttered dormer windows on the yard side with the whole place divided into three by two dividing walls. This did not suit us as we needed the whole ground floor space clear. One wall contained a chimney stack which made things more difficult.

We only had a weekly tenancy and in those days there was no security of tenure for business tenants: All the landlord had to do was give you a week's notice and you had to be out within the week. Even so, we set to with a will!

The two dividing walls and chimney stack up to first floor ceiling level had to be removed and supported by steel girders. All the steel was bought from Thomas Hill, scrap metal merchants. The price was ten shillings (fifty pence) per hundredweight and we transported it all on the flat platform of the B.S.A. outfit. In addition two girders were put in the frontage: One for a large steel framed window, again from Thomas Hill, and the other for large double doors.

Next, the whole floor area had to be dug out, layers of hard-core put in place and finally concreted with all the mixing done by hand. Again all materials transported by the B.S.A. outfit but this time with an open top packing case bolted to the platform. The yard also had to be concreted by the same method.

The only "amenity" was an outside tap so we had to install sewage piping to connect to the main sewer and install a toilet and wash basin. No gas or electricity either so we had to install that, too. All this was undertaken as a part-time project so it was a major undertaking for us which was to take us years but fortunately many of our motorcycling friends were happy to lend a hand. Among them was Harry Oulsnam who rode a late thirties 350 A.J.S.. Harry was a cheerful character, another engineer, who looked like Hoagy Carmichael. Hoagy was one of the great songwriters with such hits as "Stardust" to his credit. Want to know what Hoagy and Harry looked like? Look at "To Have and Have Not" when it next appears on T.V. ....as it surely will! This was a follow up to "Casablanca", though nothing could successfully follow that. It was, however, the first time that Bacall and Bogart appeared together and Hoagy was the cafe pianist.

Another great friend and willing helper was Vic Parker, another cheery chappie. Vic rode a 1933 350 A.J.S.. with sloping forward engine. Now A.J.S. have always been one of the great manufacturers but the early thirties was a low point in design for them. Sloping engines were in vogue to obtain the lowest possible

Chapter Twenty Nine
The Die is Cast.

In 1947 the "Direction of Labour Order" could no longer hold us at RR so T and I made the momentous and long-awaited decision to give in our notice at Rolls Royce and abandon what were already beginning to look like promising careers. So the die was cast and life was to take on an entirely new direction: It would never be the same again.

"Work is more fun than fun" said Noel Coward but up to the time that I started up in business work could hardly have been so described. At Fletcher's it was very hard work indeed in conditions that would be considered totally unacceptable today, relieved only by the pleasant characters of my fellow workers. Nothing there could be described as "fun"!

The drawing office was an enormous improvement but, once again, the fun element was conspicuous by its absence! When I joined Rolls Royce Technical staff I was getting warmer! Decent conditions, excellent, intelligent fellow workers, work of absorbing interest at one of the world's greatest engineering companies with the bonus of a marvellous, fair minded and ever helpful boss in the form of fellow motorcycle enthusiast, Chris Harrison. More fun than fun? Not quite, but getting close!

In business at last and, yes, work was more fun than fun. My work was my hobby at last: How many people are fortunate enough to make such a claim? A pleasure to buy, a pleasure to sell and a pleasure to deal with fellow motorcyclists, at least, most of the time! Obviously not every hour of every day was a pleasure and there were problems to solve, some of them very difficult indeed but, in the main, "more fun than fun".

Although we were very interested in sales and had already done a considerable amount of buying and selling we considered that repairs would provide basic bread and butter and in addition, be the key to better sales.

We asked ourselves how we could obtain a competitive edge and attract customers away from the established dealers in the town with showrooms to display their bikes? The answer was the better preparation and backup we could provide with our up to date workshop so our slogan had to be "The Finest Motorcycle Workshop in Derby".

Deciding on a name we considered "Mactun" which would combine our two names but thought "ton" would be a better ending, hence "Macton Motors".

It is difficult today to appreciate the importance of motorcycles and motorcycle combinations in those days: Just before the War there had been about 400,000 motorcycles and combinations on the road and about two million cars. In 1948 there were 500,000 motorcycles and combinations and three million cars. In 1997 there were twenty three million cars and only a handful of motorcycles.

Our repair charge was seven shillings an hour (thirty five pence)...when we could get it! This comprised three shillings we paid in wages, three shillings for overheads and one shilling profit. To take out a set of motorcycle front forks, straighten them after crash damage and replace them we charged thirty shillings (one pound fifty pence).

We got off to a good start because in the immediate post war world the pent-up demand ensured booming business. Servicemen returning from the War all wanted motorcycles and we were in the right place at the right time: Something that doesn't always happen in life! In the first year or so we employed several men though not all at the same time: Good guys every one and all motorcycle enthusiasts.

One of the very first was Charlie Gatenby. Now Charlie was a Rolls Royce engineer and first class motorcycle mechanic. He had, in fact, started in the motorcycle business part time before the War. He had restored a 1932 overhead camshaft Norton which

204

went like a bomb and succeeded in terrifying me once when I was persuaded to ride pillion, but never again! Charlie's riding style was distinctive: we called it the "Gato crouch" together with the ever present "Gato scowl".

At the same time as Charlie, Reg Thornhill worked for us. Another old motorcycling friend and ex-RR man. Reg had a lovely 1938 600cc Ariel Square Four, a beautiful machine. He once lent it to me for a trip to Rhyl and back and what a memorable ride it was: Smooth four cylinder power, sparkling performance and excellent handling. Reg also bought a mid 1930's 250 MOV Velocette to ride over the Derbyshire trials country with us. Reg was an extremely nice chap but not really a fast enough worker to make motorcycle repairs pay.

Ron Page was another of our mechanics whom we had poached from Palins, Derby's biggest motorcycle dealer holding all the plum agencies except B.S.A.. Ron was from Lincoln and had bought a Triumph Speed Twin new from West's of Lincoln in 1938. A one hundred percent enthusiast who lived and breathed motorcycles. He was married with a little girl always referred to as "Our Diane!

Bill Roe was another one: An exceptionally nice type of man, older than us and Chairman of the Pathfinders Motorcycle Club, of which we were all enthusiastic members. Bill bought a 250 MOV Velocette which he converted to trials specification to join us in tackling the Derbyshire trials sections.

Apprentices were an essential part of Macton Motors and over the years we had every possible type of youngster: Good, bad, indifferent, diabolical!

The old saying, whether by William Shakespeare, Confucius or Joe Bloggs, I cannot say, but it goes like this: "If you've got a lad, you've got a man. If you've got two lads, you've got half a man. If you've got three lads, you haven't got a man at all"

We were to discover, from experience, how true this saying was!

When any youngster leaves school to start work it is a tremendous change in his lifestyle. Instead of a fairly relaxed routine with modest hours and the choice of whether to work or not, he is suddenly plunged into the world of work. No chance now to take it easy and the hours are much longer, too.

We started work at 9am, half an hour for lunch to finish at 5.30pm. A tea break mid morning and mid afternoon which was supposed to be ten minutes but if stretched to 15, that was fine. We always felt that these breaks were never time wasted as it gave everyone a most welcome breather. We closed Wednesday afternoons but were open all day Saturday, finishing at 5pm.

So that week's work was very hard going for the newcomers and towards the end of a working day they were visibly wilting!

For a start, of course, a newcomer did not get paid much, nor was he worth much! It took a long time to train a youngster to earn his keep and how good or poor he was depended on his application...or lack of it. Those that were never going to make it found out fairly soon and were off to try their hands at another line of work. The good ones, engineering-minded and motorcycle-minded, got on and made good progress.

It was very rewarding indeed to train a youngster who was keen as mustard and eager to learn but the flip side was that such youngsters would often leave for pastures newer and greener! Over the years we turned out some tip top talent.

To find a good motorcycle mechanic was another thing, as first class men were as scarce as gold dust. Over the years we were very fortunate and employed some excellent men. Once again, you could have a really excellent man but he would decide to leave at the height of the season when you were snowed under with work. What could you do about it? Absolutely nothing! That was one of the hazards of being in business!

In the 1947/49 period, however, we were very fortunate as far as labour was concerned.

When 1947 arrived, despite all the doom and gloom, the good news was that there was to be the T.T. in June and the Motorcycle Show at Earls Court in October. The bad news, however, was that there was to be no Motorcycle Show after all! There still would be a T.T. however.

A shortened Scottish Six Days Trial was held but instead of starting at Edinburgh it was centred on Fort William. The superlative trials rider, Hugh Viney won on his Works A.J.S. and Harold Taylor, despite having only one leg, won the sidecar class.

As far as the T.T. was concerned the supercharged B.M.W.'s had outclassed the unsupercharged Nortons in 1939 but the

F.I.C.M. had banned them after the War so everyone started out level with unsupercharged engines. Omobono Tenni on his Guzzi won the Senior, Fergus Anderson, famous rider from the pre war Continental Circuses won the Junior on a Velocette and Guzzi were the first three in the Lightweight.

This was the first time that the Clubman's T.T. had been run and the Lightweight winner was Bill McVeigh of Grimsby riding a 250 Tiger 70 Triumph and entered by the Derby Pathfinders Motorcycle Club.

Ariel introduced their new 500 vertical twin late in the year and a notable milestone was the introduction of the R.A.C-A.C.U. Training Scheme.

The Training Scheme had only been running a few weeks when the Basic Petrol Ration was withdrawn on November 30th so everyone was off the road again! For our business, of course, a bitter blow that almost proved fatal!

So 1947, which had been a difficult and traumatic year ended on a downbeat.

Late 1930's Martin J.A.P. or "Speedway J.A.P." Still the basic
Speedway Rudge frame with alcohol J.A.P. engine. Identical to
the machine I rode.

(Top) Workshop completed with bikes on the ramps we made.
Excelsior Manxman in foreground. Ex-WD Matchless next, then
1938 Triumph Tiger 80. One of the girders we fitted now in place.
(Bottom) Workshop looking the opposite way, showing workshop
equipment.

Chapter Thirty
The Petrol Protest Rally

A friend of mine, a Derbyshire farmer/philosopher, once said to me "There is a fine line between profit and loss and success and failure". In 1947, however, we narrowly missed tripping over that fine line and falling flat on our faces!

We had just got the business going well and were starting to make progress when the Government hit one of its many balance of payment crises and they decided to stop petrol for private use from November 1947: This had the effect of depriving us of nearly all of our customers at a stroke.

So what could we do? The answer was twofold: Organise a nationwide Petrol Protest Rally and find some way of keeping the wolf from the door until petrol was restored.

Faced with the problem of keeping the business going when basic petrol was stopped and there was no private motoring or motorcycling we racked our brains to see what could be done.

In those days incapacitated people were not given cars but Invalid Carriages. They were tiny three wheeled contraptions with two wheels at the back and a single steerable wheel at the front. No bodywork, the driver was out there in the elements. There was no provision for anyone but the driver, of course.

They were driven by a 250 cc Villiers engine. They had no self starter so they were started by pulling a lever.

You steered them by grasping a handle with your left hand and twisted it clockwise to turn right and anticlockwise to turn left. When you first tried to steer one and attempted to master the steering you inevitably found the vehicle would leap onto the pavement.

But could some bread and butter be earned by repairing or maintaining these monstrosities? Worth a try, so we got in touch with the Ministry responsible and, yes, we were accepted as repairers and restorers. As they would have said in "Alias Smith and Jones": "Was this a good deal?".

The "Man from the Ministry" was pleasant enough and fair enough but he was governed by the most stringent rules, rigidly applied. If all government departments had been as strictly controlled the British economy would have been the wonder of the Western World.

We serviced, maintained and completely restored these machines. To have the tubular steel chassis stove-enamelled cost us £8 and we had to transport it to and from Clarkes of Nottingham to get it done. All the Ministry would pay us was £6.10. which was the maximum allowable.

Labour, too, was only chargeable at the strict times allocated for every job by the Ministry: Times we found difficult or absolutely impossible to achieve. We did make a modest mark-up on any spares, such as bearings, but "modest" was the operative word.

The Ministry then took a bold step: They introduced the new B.S.A. Invalid Carriage. This, at last, was enclosed but to get at the 250 side-valve B.S.A. engine to service it, you had to climb in between two sheet metal panels. The phrase "soul destroying" might have been coined especially to describe this operation and at the same time the Ministry decided to supply us with all materials, such as bearings, so that modest source of profit was withdrawn.

That was the last straw, draining the very last penny of profit out of the whole project. Fortunately, however, just when we were at our wits end, basic petrol was restored and we thankfully abandoned the whole thing.

One good thing did come out of it: We met Mr. Woodisse of Wolverhampton who was in a very big way restoring and maintaining invalid carriages. He was very helpful indeed, giving us all the tips and information he could and supplying any spares we needed. How did he make the job pay? By dedication, hard work and economies of scale.

Another project we took on to keep the wolf from the door when petrol was stopped was the manufacture of pannier frames for Feridax Limited. In those days Feridax was probably the most prestigious accessory supplier in the motorcycle business and Tich Allen was their Midlands representative.

In the 1930's motorcycles were fitted with a sprung saddle and separate pillion seat but in the mid 1930's Velocette fitted a rudimentary dualseat to one of their racing motorcycles, promptly dubbed "The Loch Ness Monster" by Velocette's masterly wordsmith, Harold Willis. Harold, during his lifetime, invented a whole vocabulary of terms for mechanical components of which the enduring "Double Knocker" for twin overhead camshaft is probably the best known.

Jim Ferriday was a brilliant businessman who took note of the Loch Ness Monster and designed dualseats to be sold to the public before the War. I believe I am correct in saying that the word "Dualseat" was coined by Jim Ferriday. After the War the Feridax Dualseats were re-designed and improved and Jim's "Feridax" company went from strength to strength.

Discussing with Tich the problem we faced when petrol was withdrawn he suggested to us the possibility of manufacturing easily fitted motorcycle pannier frames as he was sure there would be a demand. They were to be universal fitting to any machine by means of steel clips, like hinges, clamped to mudguard rims. If we could make them, Feridax would buy them.

We designed a jig and got to work making them and although it was none too profitable it did bring in some badly needed bread and butter until petrol returned.

Our first step had been to get in touch with The Motor Cycle and Motorcycling to see if they would support us in organising a nationwide petrol protest rally. The answer was "Yes" so we went down to see them to explain what we had in mind. We wanted them to help us to organise a series of petrol protest rallies throughout the country and to urge every reader to write protest letters to their MP's.

First line of attack was the Motorcycle Clubs: Would they mobilise their members and organise protest meetings locally which would, of course, be open to everyone who wanted to protest? They all agreed and I travelled to Clubs all over the

211

Country to talk to them and explain what was required. I went as far North as Sheffield and as far South as Sanderstead, Surrey. Public meetings were held, too, to protest and organise Protest Rallies, all to be held on the same day.

The country was short of dollars to pay for the War despite everything possible being exported under the slogan "Export Or Die". But, of course, when dollars ran short a simple solution was to stop private petrol.

Everyone lobbied their MP's and we organised a deputation to meet George Brown M.P. and a government minister, to plead our case. Our local Motorcycle Club, the Derby Pathfinders, enthusiastically took part and the local meeting was held at Wingfield Park. The meetings all over the country were held on the same day, gaining massive support with extensive news and newsreel coverage. No TV in those days. I, and others, addressed the meeting asking for more support, more lobbying.

So did we do any good? Hard to say but we did put our case forcefully to the Government so perhaps petrol was restored sooner than it would otherwise have been.

So how did we survive this bleak period in business? Not without great difficulty! We held onto our staff as long as we could but eventually most had to go and this was a great wrench. T and I soldiered on, just managing to keep the wolf from the door, though he came disconcertingly close and you can still see his claw marks on the gate at 25 Melbourne Street!

In Spring 1948 it was announced that basic petrol would return on June 1st. Not a lot, as Paul Daniels would have said: Nine gallons for six months under 250cc and thirteen gallons for six months over 250cc but we would all be back on the road again after a dreadfully long haul.

We were able to get under way again, to our great relief, and as business developed it brought home to us what we had realised all along: The real money was in sales rather than repairs but to really expand the sales side we had to have shop premises.

Shop premises, too, were also in very short supply but we were fortunate to find 178 Normanton Road, not far from Melbourne Street. Only the lock up shop was available as the rear and upper part of the premises were occupied, but this suited us well enough as we had the nearby workshop premises in Melbourne Street. I have an idea that the rent was £1 a week. We took over, redecorated inside and out and were ready to move into a higher gear with a showroom to display bikes for sale

At the start of the New Year A.J.S. announced their 350cc 7R overhead camshaft "Boy Racer" and Triumphs introduced their production racer, the Triumph Grand Prix, based on the Ernie Lyons Manx Grand Prix winner.

B.S.A. brought out their immortal 125 Bantam and at the other end of the scale Vincent launched the magnificent 1,000cc Black Shadow.

When the T.T. came round Omobono Tenni was in the lead again on his Guzzi vee-twin until engine trouble put him out and Bell, Doran and Weddell were one, two, three on Nortons but an amazing effort was Geoff Murdoch in fourth place on a 350 A.J.S. 7R. In the Junior it was Frith and Bob Foster on Velocettes with Bell and Lockett following on Nortons. In the Lightweight it was the immortal Maurice Cann on a Guzzi, Roland Pike on his Pike Rudge in second place, another remarkable achievement, and in third place D. St. John Beasley on one of the pre War overhead camshaft Excelsiors.

Sadly Omobono Tenni was killed in practising for the Swiss Circuit de Berne. Despite his age, 43, he was still a superb, competitive, rider who had started riding for Guzzi in 1934.

At Bonneville Roland Free rode his Vincent Black Lightning at 150.313mph to claim the US National Record and in Belgium Milhough, also riding a Vincent, took a series of world sidecar records. Solo he achieved 143mph.

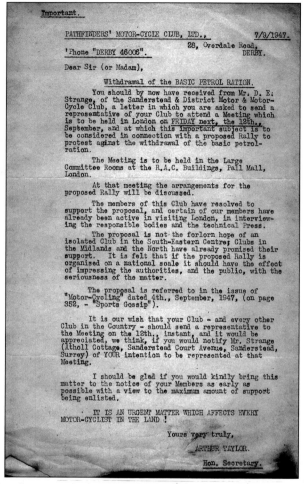

PATHFINDERS' MOTOR-CYCLE CLUB, LTD.,　　　　7/9/1947.

'Phone "DERBY 46006".

28, Overdale Road,
DERBY.

Dear Sir (or Madam),

Withdrawal of the BASIC PETROL RATION.

You should by now have received from Mr. D. E. Strange, of the Sanderstead & District Motor & Motor-Cycle Club, a letter in which you are asked to send a representative of your Club to attend a Meeting which is to be held in London on FRIDAY next, the 12th., September, and at which this important subject is to be considered in connection with a proposed Rally to protest against the withdrawal of the basic petrol-ration.

The Meeting is to be held in the Large Committee Rooms at the R.A.C. Buildings, Pall Mall, London.

At that meeting the arrangements for the proposed Rally will be discussed.

The members of this Club have resolved to support the proposal, and certain of our members have already been active in visiting London, in interviewing the responsible bodies and the technical Press.

The proposal is not the forlorn hope of an isolated Club in the South-Eastern Centre; Clubs in the Midlands and the North have already promised their support. It is felt that if the proposed Rally is organised on a national scale it should have the effect of impressing the authorities, and the public, with the seriousness of the matter.

The proposal is referred to in the issue of "Motor-Cycling" dated 4th., September, 1947, (on page 352, - "Sports Gossip").

It is our wish that your Club - and every other Club in the Country - should send a representative to the Meeting on the 12th., instant, and it would be appreciated, we think, if you would notify Mr. Strange (Atholl Cottage, Sanderstead Court Avenue, Sanderstead, Surrey) of YOUR intention to be represented at that Meeting.

I should be glad if you would kindly bring this matter to the notice of your Members as early as possible with a view to the maximum amount of support being enlisted.

IT IS AN URGENT MATTER WHICH AFFECTS EVERY MOTOR-CYCLIST IN THE LAND !

Yours very truly,

ARTHUR TAYLOR.

Hon. Secretary.

The business was just getting on its feet in 1947 when the Government hit yet another dollar crisis and banned private motoring and motorcycling. T and I decided to organise a nationwide petrol protest rally. He held the fort while I visited motorcycle clubs throughout the country to enlist support. The rallies were held in different parts of the country though petrol was still stopped! Perhaps, however, our efforts got it restored more quickly than if we had done nothing.

September, 1947.

The WITHDRAWAL of the BASIC PETROL RATION ALLOWANCE.

To :- HIS MAJESTY'S GOVERNMENT.

The **PETITION** of the British Motor-Cyclists

Sheweth :-

(1) That the withdrawal is likely to have an adverse effect on the morale of the working-men, many of whom find in motor-cycling their principal means of relaxation, holiday transport, etc. and who are, at this grave turning-point in the welfare of the Nation asked to give their maximum assistance in production and who are called upon to make an effort no less in importance than that which was required during the War ;

(2) That the public will be forced to make use of an already over-burdened transport system which, it is known, is quite unable to cope with present demands ;

(3) That the withdrawal is certain to seriously affect the small business-man who has, in many instances, invested his savings (including his War gratuities) in the setting up of a motor-cycle agency and repair business ;

(4) That it will lead to stagnation in the design and development of motor-cycles – an important matter when it is remembered that the export of British motor-cycles has been the means of very greatly assisting our overseas trade and the raising of further dollar funds ;

(5) That the results of the withdrawal will be beneficial only to our foreign competitors who will be left to develop their markets freely whilst the British manufacturer will be unable to test his products through participation in reliability trials and racing in this Country ;

(6) That our export trade will be adversely affected by an increase in prices consequent upon the lack of home markets for our machines ;

(7) That the withdrawal will effect a net saving in dollars too small to compensate for the losses involved, including the loss of revenue in the form of motor-vehicle licence fees and taxes ;

(8) That from the point of view of the Clubs the withdrawal means the complete cessation of their activities after a period of several years of hard work in re-forming Clubs whose existence was seriously affected by the War and whose members gave their full-time devotion to the National effort at that time.

Wherefore your Petitioners humbly pray that you will give grave consideration to the effect of the decision to withdraw the basic petrol-allowance and will decide to continue the basic petrol allowance for the motor-cyclist.

Signature	*Address*	*Registration Number of vehicle (if any)*

A petition that we in Derby had printed and distributed nationwide. Many thousands of signatures were obtained.

Ex-WD motorcycle value in 1947 from Marble Arch.

Chapter Thirty One
Really Breaking Into the Bike Business

We had the finest motorcycle workshop in Derby and a showroom to go with it so the next step was to put some new machines in it for sale.

In the immediate post war world the slogan was "Export or die". Export was the first priority to bring in much needed foreign currency, especially dollars, so the majority of motorcycles that were manufactured were exported. The small proportion that were supplied to the home market were easily sold by established dealers so no manufacturer had the need to appoint new dealers.

The answer for us, then, was a sub-agency from an established dealer in the town and the decision whether or not to appoint a sub-dealer was left entirely to them, not the manufacturers.

When we approached any of the established dealers they realised only too well that we were fanatical motorcycle enthusiasts who lived and breathed motorcycles. Appoint us and they were appointing opposition who could be more successful than they were so the answer had to be "NO". We had no chance!

The biggest dealer in the town both before and after the war was Herbert Palin, "Derby's first expert under A.C.U. rules" as proclaimed on his headed paper. He had large modern premises and held all the plum agencies: A.J.S., Matchless, Douglas, Sunbeam, Norton, Royal Enfield and more. No way would he appoint us, or anyone else, as a sub-agent.

By that time he was a crusty old timer who sat behind the counter, an unsmiling patriarch. You could well have been forgiven for thinking that his features had been hewn from Derbyshire Gritstone. If you went in to ask for motorcycle spares his unfailing riposte was "Wheresyerpattern?" I'm sure I once caught the glimmer of a smile flickering across his face, but it could have been a trick of the light!

On one occasion I walked up to the counter, put on my brightest smile and said "Good morning, Mr. Palin". The response was a stony stare that Coleridge's ancient mariner would have envied! No reply was forthcoming for such irrelevant nonsense! His right hand man was G.K. "Mac" Church. Mac had been in the motorcycle business all his life and had worked for Palin for many years but, of course, as we were regarded as potentially dangerous opposition we got neither encouragement or help from Mac. His loyalty had to be to his employer.

It was usual for a dealer to hold a number of agencies but not in the case of Triumph and B.S.A. or, for that matter, Velocette, though Velocette were a much smaller outfit. The Triumph dealer was E. O. Blacknell. His principal business was in Arkwright Street, Nottingham so he had a manager in his Derby shop on Osmaston Road.

Before the War, W.H. Jones had quite a thriving business and had kept his shop going through the War years by selling objets d'art. Unfortunately his better agencies in the 1930's had gone out of business during the War, for example O. K. Supreme and New Imperial, but he did manage to retain James after the War.

He had also held the Ariel agency and I remember seeing the first post war Ariel in his shop but I understand that when the Ariel representative saw it among the bric a brac he immediately withdrew the Ariel agency from Jones and gave it to Palin. If this was, in fact, the case it was very unfair on Jones who had been given no opportunity to get properly started again in the motorcycle business.

Freddie Craner on London Road had taken on the Velocette agency. Freddie was a larger than life character who had ridden in the T.T. and entered his own team of 500cc vee-twin James motorcycles in the International Six Days Trial in the early 1930's.

Freddie was the man whose vision and enterprise created the Donington Park racing circuit. Realising the potential in the early 1930's, Freddie went to see the owner and persuaded him to allow a race meeting to be held there. It was a great success and from then on it went from strength to strength.

The new motorcycle for everyone, the revolutionary almost silent LE with its horizontally-opposed, twin-cylinder 150cc side-valve engine was sold by Craner's.

The most important single agency was, without doubt, B.S.A. with their comprehensive range of models. They were sold by Mr. and Mrs. Lilley at Ingles Garage, The Cavendish, Derby. Ingles had started a B.S.A. agency at Smalley near Derby before moving to Derby itself. Ken Lilley had come from Yorkshire to work at Ingles and had married Miss Ingle.

Mrs. Lilley was a lovely person but Ken Lilley was a bluff Yorkshireman who definitely regarded us as potential opposition, not to be helped! No chance of a B.S.A. sub-agency!

Wilemans had been in business before the War in a small way selling spares and second-hand motorcycles. It was run by Bernard and Ken Wileman; we got on very well with them and found them unfailingly helpful. Both had served in the War, Bernard in the Army and Ken in the RAF

The biggest dealer in second hand machines was Dawsons Motors, Traffic Street, Derby. The Dawson brothers were from Nottingham where they had a thriving motorcycle business which had kept going during the War repairing military motorcycles and selling second-hand machines.. After the War they bought Ex.WD. machines by the hundred, if not by the thousand, which were sold by both Nottingham and Derby depots together, of course, with all kinds of used machines. The Derby branch was run by another Yorkshireman.

A throwback from the 1920's was a peculiar shop on the corner of Normanton Road and Mill Hill Lane, run by a father and his bachelor son. Both seemed like very old timers to us in those days. Their premises were crammed with motorcycles and even a few small cars with their Normanton Road window displaying Crown Derby China.

Their prices were always impossibly high and though their stock had been there since the 1930's... or before, I never remember them actually selling anything. The older man told me that in the early 1920's he had the biggest stock of second-hand motorcycles in the Midlands. If this was the case I'm sure that some of them were still there.

The original B.S.A. agents in Derby were Kay and Scampton in Sadlergate. They were still in business after the War and still held a B.S.A. agency, though sales must have dwindled to practically nothing by then and they kept going by selling bicycles and accessories.

Tom Kay and the strangely named Tertius Scampton had been fellow cycle enthusiasts who had graduated to the new motorcycles when they started to take over. Tom Kay had left many years ago to successfully enter the Motor Trade in Derby, acquiring the Singer agency for his premises on Ashbourne Road. Tertius Scampton continued in Sadlergate.

Another "character" in the motorcycle business was Tom Ward of Wilfred Street, a Yorkshireman who had worked at Scott's, Shipley way back when. He had a flourishing mail order business supplying Scott spares and overhauling Scott engines and gearboxes.

Maurice Patey was a great friend of his, as was Arthur Battelle. Arthur, in fact, managed to find some time to do some work for him. Very few people could match Tom's knowledge and expertise on Scotts.

Samways of Nuns Street were mostly concerned with cycles before the War, though they did sell some motorcycles. After the War they got more involved in the motorcycle world. They had an excellent reputation for fair dealing and everyone spoke well of them.

Minions had been in business before the War, mostly in the cycle trade. They had a small shop in one of the streets behind London Road but after the War they were to go over to motorcycles and eventually open much larger premises on London Road.

So that was the picture in the motorcycle trade in the immediate post war period: As far as agencies or sub-agencies were concerned it was a closed shop for interlopers like us! If, however, that was the bad news, the good news was that there was an enormous demand for motorcycles: Time for action!

Pride and Clarke still offering fantastic value for money. Five gallons of oil still under £1.

(Top) 1937 350cc Manx Norton with many modifications carried out by Geoff Nantes. Engine modified as a replica of Johnny Lockett's 1939 Francis Beart tuned 350. Modifications included a "square" head, additional barrel finning, sodium-cooled, exhaust valve, increased capacity oil pumps and much more. Originally rigid frame but rear springing designed and fitted by Geoff. We completely stripped and rebuilt it, but not the engine, in 1947.

(Bottom) 1936 500cc International Norton. We completely reconditioned it in 1947. Before overhaul the machine had been ridden to destruction so we rebuilt everything, including engine and gearbox. I remember riding it in third gear at 89mph on the Burnaston straight. This picture was taken a year after restoration.

Chapter Thirty Two
Sales and Salesmanship.

"Shopkeeper must have smiling face" Old Chinese saying.

I have always been very interested in selling and how to sell. "But isn't it dreadfully vulgar to attempt to sell anything to anyone?" Lady Bracknell would have said. No, it is not! It is, in fact, of vital importance that goods are sold.

Imagine a huge factory working at full blast: Presses thump, lathes spin, furnaces roar, designers design, draughtsmen draw: But it is all completely pointless and will grind to a halt *unless something is sold.* Everything depends on sales.

In our case we did not have the responsibility of keeping a factory in production but we did have to keep our business going and without sales our business would have folded

I have already mentioned Joe Utting's sales idea without using capital: Make a sale having first agreed with the owner to go 50/50 on any profit over the price he wants and I have successfully used this system many times.

At Rolls Royce, Sinfin, was a diminutive Scotsman named "Jock" Brown, a driver not an engineer. A very likeable chap and a natural salesman. In those days of post war shortages he would manage to get hold of all sorts of goods in short supply and sell them round the plant.

He had been asked to obtain something for a potential customer which he managed to secure at a reasonable price but when he offered it to the man it was turned down: The Scotsman was visibly annoyed.

He knew, of course, that I was also keen to sell and he said to me "If you attempt to pull off a sale, a sale you really need to make and your offer is rejected you will be bound to be annoyed but *never let the customer know.* I can sometimes let my exasperation show and this is a fault: Make sure you avoid it." I have always tried to do so, often with great difficulty and on rare occasions I haven't managed it! The advice, however, is absolutely right.

When we started in business we obtained an agency for motorcycle insurance with Invincible Policies and the local manager was a Leicester man named Charlie Reasby. (Charlie had shaken Charlie Dodson's hand after he had won the 1929 T.T. on a Sunbeam). Charlie was also a very likeable man who was a natural salesman.

He said to me "Never ask a question that invites a negative reply. Always ensure a positive reply. For example do not ask a question starting "You wouldn't have..." For example, "You wouldn't have change for a pound, would you?" This invites "No" for an answer. What you should say is "Would you have change for a pound, please?" or "Could you possibly change a pound?" Both these questions put "Yes" on the recipient's lips."

I have never forgotten this and would never say "You wouldn't have...." I tried for years to teach Edna this but with no result! She always starts such a question with "You wouldn't have...."

Now for a few tips of my own: Someone asks "Will you do me a favour?" As you well know, your immediate reaction is a scowl followed by a snarled "Worrissit?" Negative!

If someone asks "Will you do me a favour" you immediately *smile* and instantly reply "I will if I can". Positive! It does *not* commit you to anything yet you do not instantly dub yourself a scowler and snarler!

If anyone *does* ask you that question it is usually something that you would be very pleased to do anyway or would be happy to do to oblige so there is no need for a negative reaction.

If you want to sell you must be positive and not only have a smiling face but a smiling telephone voice. Once again a snarl or growl will not do. Put the caller at his ease with a pleasant, smiling voice.

You must have confidence in yourself and never forget that the only person who can make you feel inferior is you! Never forget the old Bing Crosby song "Accentuate the positive, eliminate the negative."

When talking to a customer smile, be positive, avoid controversy, get on his side and that will mean he will get on *your* side. So is the customer always right? Well, not necessarily, but if you convince him he's wrong, you've lost the sale!

Whatever you do, avoid words or phrases that will automatically put the customer's back up. A well known phrase that I have learned *not* to use when disagreeing with a customer is to say "With respect..." It invariably tends to strike the wrong note. The customer does *not* feel you "respect" him because, after all, you are disagreeing with him! Negative. Avoid.

Another phrase you must avoid is "I would argue that......" Another emotive word: Argue implies disagreement. Avoid. There are many other such negative examples and they do not just apply to selling but to everyday life.

One principle to which I have always adhered is "Never tell a lie when trying to sell." Doctor Johnson said: *"It is the peculiar condition of falsehood to be equally detested by the good and the bad."* Still just as true today. Tell a lie and it will always trip you up in the end even after you have made the sale. It is not your function to tell the customer you know and it is perfectly legitimate *not* to tell him *everything*, but lies are unacceptable.

For example we once bought a machine with a gearbox that had constantly given trouble despite numerous attempts by well meaning "experts" to repair it. We stripped it and carefully rebuilt it and from then on it was perfectly sound, never giving the new owner a moment's trouble.

What, however, if he had been told when he was considering buying it. "The gearbox has been constantly going wrong but it is repaired now." The answer is that he would never have bought it.

Now I am not, for one moment, saying that you should sell a car or motorcycle with a gearbox you know to be faulty but if the job has been done properly it is perfectly legitimate *not* to tell the customer *all you know* about its past history.

Some years ago when we were M.A.A. members they attempted to insist that all second-hand cars and motorcycles offered for sale by members should have a list attached to them listing all the work that had been done to make the vehicle saleable. Absolute nonsense as it would have put any customer off buying. In the end they had to drop the silly scheme.

Throughout my selling career I have been certain that if the customer wanted and needed the machine I had to offer it was up to me to do my best to sell it to him rather than leave it to one of my competitors.

Hard sell? An emotive phrase and not an exact description anyway. If the customer feels that he is being subjected to a "hard sell" technique it will immediately put his back up and stop the sale. But it is up to you to do your utmost to pull off that sale.

I have been fortunate in selling and have achieved a measure of success. Obviously you cannot be successful every time but if I failed to make a sale that I felt I should have pulled off I would go over the whole conversation in my mind to see if I could have done better.

Were there any signals I should have picked up? Did I say something that jarred, struck a wrong note? Did I miss an opportunity to push a feature that would have appealed to the customer? There is usually something to be learned.

(Top) Much modified Scott combination that started out as a 1929 model. We completely rebuilt the whole outfit in 1948.
(Bottom) 1938 500cc Triumph Speed Twin.
Another totally worn out machine that we rebuilt completely in 1948. We also fitted Stan Burnett's Ex WD Matchless telescopic forks, modifying the Triumph front wheel to suit. Photograph taken after it had been ridden for 4,500 miles.

(Top) Outside the Druid Hotel Llanferres during a day spent riding over the Clwydian Range. Maurice "Pate" Patey on his 350 Douglas, T on his 500 Scott, me on my 1938 350 Triumph Tiger 80.

(Bottom) Dump. The 1932 Raleigh three wheeler van that replaced the 1927 B.S.A. and sidecar.

Chapter Thirty Three
Objective Moel Fammau

But that period up to 1948 was a happy time despite all problems and one of our greatest pleasures was for a crowd of us to ride over to Rhyl, all stay at Stella Maris, and ride over the Clwydian Range.

During the War Douglas Cartwright had been a sergeant in the Royal Corps of Signals stationed at Prestatyn, training motorcyclists and if ever a man was born to ride motorcycles, that man was Doug Cartwright. After the War he had stayed in Rhyl and started a motorcycle repair business with his pal Wally. They worked in a small garage at the end of Gronant Street, Rhyl.

Doug was married with a young family but whenever we could persuade him to take a day off he would take us to the Clwydian Range and show us the routes he had used in training Army motorcyclists. Doug would ride all kinds of dilapidated and unlikely motorcycles on every type of terrain: On one occasion he rode a very well worn 1931 500 Ariel with the horrible near horizontal cylinder.

One of his routes was "Left hand bend" near Llanferres: You would ride up an incredibly steep slope with a stone wall running straight up the hillside on your right. At the top the stone wall turned abruptly left and ran parallel to the valley floor. The only way to go at the top was an acute left hand bend with a steep drop below. You then continued along the wall until you reached open hillside beyond. That left hand turn with the drop below you was hair raising until you got the hang of it.

Another of Doug's party tricks was "The impossible ascent". You would start from a standstill with a small hillock ahead, accelerate hard over it then hurtle up a near vertical climb that was impossible to surmount. At the very moment that your exhausted steed finally ran out of breath you would quickly lay it down onto the hillside with the footrest acting as an anchor. You were, of course, terrified of shooting backwards out of control.

Once anchored, however, you could pivot the machine round, point it downhill and quickly, very quickly, remount with the exhaust valve lifter raised. You would, of course, be in bottom gear and with the raised exhaust lifter you had a very effective brake but without locking the rear wheel. You would then make it safely to the bottom then round again for another try!

After having tackled this hill a number of times we got really good at it, even using Ex-WD Matchlesses and Ariels, but I cannot see how you would tackle it with today's bikes, even specialised trials machines. Surely they are much too high and you must have fixed, not folding, footrests. They are also mostly two-strokes today and you need a four stroke with an exhaust lifter to get down without locking the rear wheel. Having said that, watching today's trails riders on today's machines they seem to be able to make them do everything but talk, so perhaps they would find it perfectly possible!

But those days when a group of us rode over the Clwydian Range were absolutely marvellous: We would ride to Bodfari then up the Wrexham Road for two or three miles, right onto a narrow uphill road and then at the top a vast open area that had been churned up by tanks in training. This was Moel y Parc, the Park Mountain.

We would then ride over the top of the hills through all kinds of terrain and at mid-day head downhill for lunch at the Druid Hotel Llanferres. After a marvellous meal, back again via "Left hand bend" up onto the tops and on to the monument at the top of Moel Fammau (pronounced Vamma), the highest point on the Clwydian Range.

We would ride all day and when it was time to head for home we would head down the mountainside, reasoning that we would, sooner or later, be bound to encounter a road.

Riding through the heather covered hillside you would get heather trapped against the exhaust pipe with that distinctive woodsmoke-sweet smell of burning heather. Years later, deerstalking in Scotland and lighting a heather fire to signal the ponyman, that unique scent would instantly transport me in spirit to those days on the Clwydian Range.

Doug told us of a motorcyclist of unique talent that he had trained. His name? Geoff Duke! "Watch him, he will go far in motorcycling" said Doug. Geoff Duke was, of course, to go on to be one of the most brilliant racing motorcyclists of all time.

One summer holiday we had arranged to ride over to Rhyl with a motorcycling friend named Jim Staff. Jim was older and more experienced than us and rode a 1927 1,000cc Brough Superior S.S.100 overhead valve vee-twin in excellent order. Now it would be worth at least £40,000, possibly very much more. (I recently saw a 1930 example advertised for £50,000).

We used to cruise our 350's and 500's at 60/65 mph, far faster than normal family cars of that era, but would we be able to keep up with Jim, a seasoned motorcyclist, with his 100mph Brough? Discussing our proposed cruising speed with Jim brought the reply "At 60mph the telegraph posts seem to stand still!"

What could it mean? T and I puzzled about it but the conclusion was clear: We were talking to a formidable rider.

The day of departure finally arrived and we all set off together. Jim had his wife on the pillion, but it appeared to be Jim, not the telegraph posts, that were standing still!

I suppose Jim did touch 50mph on occasion but on every bend, and there were many of them, Jim struggled round like a man trying to stay on the back of a bucking broncho! At "The Red Fox" Alpraham we could stand it no longer so we pulled in and told Jim we were heading on and leaving him behind.

We had arranged to take Jim onto the Clwydian Range: Cruelty, I know, because the Brough was totally unsuitable, but at the time we had arranged it we were under the impression that Jim could ride anything anywhere. At the top of Moel y Parc on the area churned up by tanks, Jim had to admit defeat!

The greatest concerted attack on the Clwydian Range was in 1948, not long after basic petrol was restored. T and I, accompanied by Vic Parker, Alf Jeffery, Bill Roe, Harry Oulsnam, Peter Stewart and Charlie Gatenby all rode over to Rhyl to stay at Stella Maris. All free of charge as always and all of us made welcome. Many years later, T was to say to me "Your mother was a good sport". How true this was and how we always take our parents so much for granted!

On the run over we hit that lovely S bend just beyond Northop. We stopped and went back again several times... great fun. Charlie, in particular, enjoyed it immensely so henceforth it was named "The Gato Bend".

I also took them to the challenging series of bends I had discovered in my Model X Triumph days. They were on the bottom road out of Denbigh, a winding uphill climb over the river bridge with the Welsh name Pont yr allt Gogh, the red bridge over the stream. Cheerfully Anglicised by our Derbonians to Pont Ralph Cork! Everyone was introduced to this and, once again, we thoroughly enjoyed hurtling up and down these marvellous bends. They were also introduced to the Clwydian Range and, of course, Left Hand Bend and The Impossible Ascent. We all had a wonderful time, not knowing that we would never again be all together at Rhyl.

This visit was also very important for a reason entirely unconnected with motorcycles: I met Edna Neale, the girl I was to marry. Edna was a lovely girl, as were so many Rhyl girls, but Edna was not only vivacious and attractive but blessed with a vital personality and boundless energy. She worked as a secretary at Ribbons and Winder, income tax consultants, Rhyl and was also Junior Commandant of the Rhyl Red Cross.

She rode pillion with me over the Clwydian Range many times, both before and after we were married. She nonchalantly negotiated Left Hand Bend and tackled everything except The Impossible Ascent, which was quite impossible with a pillion passenger.

Edna was born at West Kirby on the Wirral Peninsular but had moved to Rhyl with her mother and two brothers when her stepfather died. She lived with her mother and younger brother at one of the pair of Edwardian glazed red brick houses opposite the water towers, Rhuddlan Road, Rhyl. After having met Edna I would ride over to Rhyl most weekends, starting from Derby at 5pm on Saturdays when I finished work and leaving Rhyl on Monday mornings to be back at work for mid day.

With 100 mile journeys throughout the year in all weathers it was essential to "Wrap up warm". I wore a one piece ex. RAF kapok lining under a one piece Barbour waxed cotton suit. Small towel round my neck as a seal and to soak up any rain. Flying helmet and goggles with ex. RAF lambswool lined boots, like riding boots, treated with dubbin to keep out the rain. For gloves, however, T and I were unique! First a pair of soft leather lambswool lined gauntlets, also ex-R.A.F.. Over them a pair of soft leather mittens with a multi-layered sandwich of newspaper in between. Finally, over the lot, a pair of waterproof mittens.

After all this, were your hands like hams? Yes, they were, but they kept out the cold. Operating the controls? Perfectly possible when you got used to it and on a winter's night, facing freezing rain or sleet and with a hundred miles to go you were very thankful for the warmth.

This is the only surviving page from our 1947 accounts in August 1947. Our total assets at cost amounted to £1,330 but our liabilities were £500. Petrol for private motoring was not to be restored until June 1948, a very long haul! We did survive.... just..... but it was a damned close run thing!

233

CELEBRATE THE RETURN
OF
"BASIC PETROL"
AT
MACTON MOTORS

Dance

INNES'S SALE ROOMS
BECKET STREET, DERBY
ON
FRIDAY, JULY 2nd, 1948
8 — 12

BUFFET   *SPOT PRIZES*   **TICKETS 2/6**

(Top) Shop at 178 Normanton Road Derby. A shop window at last
to display our wares: We were on our way! The bike in the window
is a 1947 B32 350cc B.S.A..
(Bottom) The dance we held to celebrate the return of basic petrol:
Those were the days, my friend........

Chapter Thirty Four
The First Post War
Motorcycle Show

The first motorcycle show since before the War was in November 1948. What an occasion it was, as before the War "The Show" at Earls Court was the highlight of the motorcycle year.

Bill Roe had a beautifully kept 1936 Standard Ten saloon and four of us went in it. T, believe it or not, elected to drive down in Dump. Must have done it for the challenge, for that it certainly was! He had intended to get up very early and start out long before us but, in the event, we passed him on the winding hill between Ticknall and Ashby. The Standard had no heater and it was very cold, but not nearly as cold as T in Dump!.

The Show was, without doubt, a revelation. Every manufacturer had his gleaming Show models on display: A new generation with their new telescopic forks.

The new, gleaming ebony and polished aluminium 1,000cc Vincent twins were essential viewing and Sunbeam offered a lighter version of the revolutionary shaft drive twin, the S.8., with B.S.A. forks and normal 19 inch wheels. Norton caused a sensation with their new Dominator Twin with plunger rear suspension. Royal Enfield threw their hat in the ring with their compact and attractive twin, though destined never to be as successful as the leading makes. This had swinging arm rear suspension. A.J.S. and Matchless had their elegantly proportioned swinging arm twins. Excellent machines that were to go from strength to strength.

In June 1948 one of the greatest post war models made its debut: The immortal B.S.A. Bantam. This was a 125cc machine which was a copy of the pre war D.K.W.. It shot to immediate popularity and was to progress to 150 and then 175cc. They sold successfully all over the world.

The sought after, but ultimately unattainable, "Holy Grail" of motorcycling was the machine for everyman. A machine that would appeal to non-motorcyclists as basic transport. It had to be quiet, economical, easy to clean and with a measure of weather protection.

During the 1930's the nearest machine to that ideal was the partially enclosed Francis Barnett "Cruiser". The lower part was enclosed by pressed steel panels and there were built in legshields. Powered by a 250 Villiers engine it was an excellent, practical machine and did fulfil most of the requirements for an everyman machine, though it never really achieved a mass market.

During the War, Velocette, who were justly famous for sporting O.H.V. or overhead camshaft sports machines, decided to make a serious attempt at capturing this hitherto elusive everyman market and after years of development the revolutionary 150cc LE was introduced in 1948. Inevitably to be called in Derbyshire the "Lee Veller"!

The LE was hailed as the answer. At last the machine for everyman had arrived. It had a 150cc horizontally-opposed, water-cooled, twin-cylinder engine set across the frame like a B.M.W. so it fulfilled the first requirement... a really quiet engine. Instead of a kick starter, it was started by pulling on a hand lever. As for comfort it was sprung front and rear with swinging arm rear suspension.

Quietness and comfort had been achieved so what about ease of cleaning? The machine was designed to be hosed down, like a motorcar. Economy? 100mpg with an oil consumption of 5,000 mpg and the modest weight of 240 pounds made it very easy to handle.

Handling, stability and adequate performance surely made it the machine for everyman, so was the Holy Grail finally within grasp? Sadly, no.

Firstly, despite extensive development, the original machines were far from trouble free and modifications galore had to be made. This inevitably blunted the impact. Problems were eventually solved and reliability achieved but the LE never attained a mass market and the Holy Grail stayed tantalisingly out of reach, where it remains to this day.

Not only was there a bewildering array of motorcycles but all the accessory and clothing manufacturers were there together with anything else connected with motorcycles. To get through it all in a day was quite impossible and the unique heat and stuffiness at Earls Court, never to be forgotten by anyone who has ever been there at Show time, made it very hard going!

We were there, however, to enjoy ourselves and see as much as we possibly could before we eventually had to climb back into Bill's car for the return journey to Derby.

The bikes that made the greatest impression on us were the Triumphs and of the whole range the 500cc Triumph Trophy was the most desirable. During the War, Triumph had made, among other things, a mobile generating set for the static charging of aircraft batteries. A normal 500cc twin bottom half was used but a new all alloy top half was fitted. In 1946 the first post-War Manx Grand Prix was won by Irishman Ernie Lyons riding a tuned version of one of these engines in a Tiger 100 frame. This was the inspiration for the Grand Prix racing Triumph and the "All rounder" Trophy model.

The Trophy was one of the last, if not *the* last of the great all-rounders: At four point five to one compression ratio you could ride it in Trials. For a fast run to the coast you changed to seven to one. Ride it in Road Races at Cadwell Park with the high compression nine to one pistons.

T decided that he must have one. I would have loved one, too, but by then I was saving to get married. Even Pate was tempted to abandon his beloved Scotts! We thought then, and I still think now, that the Triumph Trophies of that era were one of the greatest bikes of all time. T was to ride his on the road and in Trials, Scrambles, over the Clwydian Range and even, on one memorable occasion, at Cadwell.

Racing at Cadwell he shot out in front in his heat and stayed there throughout the race. This against Manx Nortons and 7R

237

A.J.S.'s. No, he didn't win the final, but that heat win was a remarkable achievement.

I restored one half a century later and even today's motorcyclists were surprised and delighted by how well it performed.

So after a marvellous day at the Show, tired and elated, we climbed back into Bill's car for the bitterly cold trip back to Derby.... **but what about poor old T in Dump?**

(Top) No, this was not one of ours! It is a 500cc Moto Guzzi **used** by the Italian Army during the War, Spring frame compared to our rigid frame machines but, surprisingly, hand gearchange. Inlet over exhaust valve engines. Arnold Tunaley owned one after the War: Goodness knows how he got hold of it!

(Bottom) The WD 350cc 3HW Triumph. we sold quite a lot of them and liked them very much indeed.

(Top) WD 350cc Velocette. Harder to obtain than most of the
other ex-WD machines but we bought and sold them when we
could. Charlie Gatenby owned an excellent example.
(Bottom) WD Triumph 3TW. 350cc Vertical twin with unit
construction three speed gearbox. Weight only 260lbs.
Unfortunately only prototypes were made and they never entered
production, but we considered it to be an ideal machine at the time
and would have loved to have owned one.

(Top) The 1948 L.E. Velocette, 150cc horizontally-opposed, unit-construction, water-cooled twin. Light, smooth, silent and a gallant attempt to grasp the Holy Grail of motorcycling: The machine for everyman with its vast sales potential. Sadly the Holy Grail proved to be out of reach, where it remains to this day. (Bottom) The 125cc B.S.A. Bantam. Originally introduced in 1948 with rigid frame it was a great success right from the start and continued for years in 150 and 175cc form. The machine illustrated is the spring frame model, late 1949.

Chapter Thirty Five
Alfred G.Baker Artisan
A Most Remarkable Derbyshire Man

Alf Baker is Derbyshire's answer to Fred Dibnah: Their personalities are entirely different but their range of interests are similar. Fred is a Bolton Steeplejack, Alf is a Derbyshire motor engineer but they are both men of steel: Steam engines, motorcycles, anything mechanical.

So why "Artisan"? Artisan is the word used to describe a skilled craftsman, still commonplace in France but virtually obsolete here. Alf trained as an auto-electrician but can tackle anything in the motor trade, ancient or modern. He has no formal qualifications but when he started in the motor trade he decided that "Artisan" was the ideal job description.

Alf has a remarkable range of interests: motorcycle enthusiast, steam engine man, historian, raconteur, dinghy sailor and yachtsman, rifle shot, hill walker, rock climber, ballroom dancer, genealogist and not least, good Samaritan. Break down 50 miles from home in freezing rain on a winter's night at am and ring Alf... he would instantly come over and get you out of trouble.

Alf's wife died of cancer leaving him to bring up two small boys on his own but despite all difficulties he managed it successfully.

So with such a range of skills and interests, is Alf a wealthy man? Sadly, no! He claims, in fact, that the Baker family motto is "No matter how bad things are, they can always get a bloody sight worse!"

Alf, like all the Bakers, is a motorcycle enthusiast and Rudges are his favourites. He still has the 1932 500 he used to ride to Snowdonia as a young man.

Alf was the last man in Derby to ride a belt drive motorcycle as normal, everyday transport. This was after the War and the bike was a 1922 500cc sidevalve Campion. There was a chain from the engine to the three speed gearbox but the drive from the gearbox to the rear wheel was by belt. Campions were local machines, manufactured in nearby Nottingham using proprietary engines. The engine in Alf's 500 was a J.A.P.. Although long since pensioned off, the bike fortunately survives.

Alf has the uncanny ability to attract trouble as effectively as a magnet attracts iron filings and it would take a book to list even a fraction of them, but let me give you a couple of examples: He was once driving a Morris Minor along Kedleston Road, Derby when the bonnet flipped up, completely blotting out his vision. Not that it mattered, because at the same moment the steering wheel came off in his hands!

Early one morning Alf started out from his home in Willington at the controls of his steam engine, heading for a steam engine rally. Suddenly the boiler gasket in front of him blew. A jet of steam and boiling water hit Alf, somersaulting him backwards off the engine and onto the road. His pal managed to leap off unscathed.

The engine trundled on happily with the camber of the road keeping the wheels against the kerb. Alf and his pal ran helplessly behind, unable to get back on board because of the escaping cascade of steam and boiling water.

Now the night before a young soldier had returned on leave from Germany and had parked his newly purchased Mercedes on the wide grass verge in front of his parents' house. The steam engine had been following the kerb until it hit a splay to a driveway so it then left the road and continued on the grass verge.

Alf and his friend watched in horror as the engine headed for the Mercedes, imagining it as pancake flat as Tom in a Tom and Jerry cartoon. The engine hit the back of the car and thankfully stalled, though it didn't do the car much good!

Another Derbyshire businessmen is Arthur Battelle from Ambaston near Shardlow, Derbyshire and although he is totally different from Alf Baker there are two major similarities: They are both motorcycle enthusiasts and "hands on" engineers.

Arthur was a Scott enthusiast. He had owned a Scott of about 1930 vintage for some time but had graduated to a very well kept original 1936 model. Just after the War I bought it from him for £70 and intended to see how it performed on the Rhyl run but not long afterwards Arthur regretted the sale of his beloved Scott and bought it back for £75. Arthur is the son of a Derbyshire tenant farmer and agricultural contractor so he was not born with a silver spoon in his mouth. He worked as a tractor mechanic and ended up working for Ford, demonstrating and showing their tractors all over Europe.

Leaving Ford he and his wife, Betty, started their own business which was brilliantly successful. Arthur was finally to become an international businessman.

When new tractors were going over to four wheel drive, Arthur realised that there would be a market for converting existing tractors. He located a firm in Italy capable of producing such conversions for Ford tractors and negotiated the British agency. This was a classic example of being in the right place at the right time and, more important, having the vision to see and the courage to grasp the opportunity.

Eventually as more and more new tractors were produced with four wheel drive and the market started to wane, Arthur sold out.

On another occasion Arthur realised that there was another gap in the market: New tractors were very expensive so could he produce tractors of his own to effect a massive saving? His answer was to strip down existing tractors to the chassis, sell off the redundant parts and rebuild and re-register the tractors as new with new engines and new chassis under his own brand.

This, too, was a success until the tractor manufacturers drastically reduced their new prices.... but what profits were they making before?

The business continues, run by his son, selling parts for both modern and vintage tractors. They arrange for obsolete parts to be manufactured all over the world.

Arthur is now a consultant on vintage tractors and along the way he has written innumerable instruction books for obsolete tractors. He has also written three books on his life with tractors, starting with "Early Years on the Tractor Seat" followed by "Country Love" and "Johnsons Farm" - romantic novels based on the life and times of a farming family from the 1880's. His objective is a trilogy of these novels following the fortunes of the same family into the twentieth century, with all the tremendous changes during that period.

(Top) 1,000cc Vincent. THE superbike of its day and still a formidable performer half a century on. The first post-war models had girder forks but the model shown is the late 1949 model with Vincent's own "Girdraulic" fork. Surprisingly light, too, compared to a modern thousand and far more handleable. Which would you prefer?

(Left) The first of the B.S.A. twins, introduced in 1947 with rigid frame. It was to continue successfully into plunger suspension then swinging arm and expanded to 650cc versions.

(Top) This is the immediate post war version of the famous Ariel Square Four, now with the Ariel telescopic fork. Still with the iron engine in 1948 but changed to alloy in 1949.
(Bottom) Sunbeam 500cc twin. Announced in 1946 but not available until 1947, it was one of the brand new post war designs. Unit construction, in line twin-cylinder, overhead- camshaft, all-alloy engine. Introduced as the S7 with huge tyres but the S8 with conventional tyres soon followed. Despite their advanced design they were never a huge success, nor were they always trouble free, but full marks for a gallant effort.

Chapter Thirty Six
Motoring Myths and Legends

Ask an old India hand and he will tell you about the Indian Rope Trick: A snake charmer plays his pipe but instead of a snake a rope emerges from the basket and unwinds skywards. Eventually he stops and a small boy climbs up the rope. When the boy reaches the top he jumps off and disappears! Now the India hand has never actually seen the Indian Rope Trick performed but he knows someone who has!

Motoring, too has its myths and surely you must have heard the Rolls Royce one? If not, here goes!

A man on holiday in a remote area of England glances at the classified adverts in the local paper where he sees the following ad. "Rolls Royce for sale £25. Telephone ....."

He rings the number and a cultured female voice tells him that the car is for sale and gives him the address. He drives up a long drive to a magnificent manor house and is courteously received by an elegant lady. She shows him the Rolls, starts it up for him and having been assured that he is completely satisfied accepts £25 in full payment and hands over the registration document.

At this point he can contain his curiosity no longer and asks why such a magnificent car was offered for sale at such a ridiculously low price. "Well," she said, "my husband has died and in his will he directed that the Rolls was to be sold and the proceeds given to his secretary."

Another motoring myth is the wooden piston: You have, of course, heard of someone who stripped an engine and found that it had a wooden piston or pistons. Like the old India hand, you have never actually seen it yourself but you know a man.....

I once knew a man who owned a Ford vee eight but frost damage had caused water to leak into one of the front cylinders. He thought of a simple solution: He removed the front pair of connecting rods and pistons and wedged two carefully fitted wooden bungs or "pistons" into the now redundant bores and ran it successfully as a six cylinder engine. So was this kind of thing the start of the "wooden piston" myth?

Since writing that, however, I have read "Fifty years on British Bikes" by George Hylands. George was an expert motorcycle mechanic and tuner. He describes how a 250 Panther was brought to him for investigation: It would run satisfactorily for a few miles and then tighten up. He removed head and barrel and was astounded to find a wooden piston. The wood used was, in fact, Lignum Vitae, so there you are! The legend has become reality.

Sawdust in gearboxes is the next well known story. In days of yore when worn straight-cut gears could create a dreadful whine I am sure that a handful of sawdust in the treacly gear oils of the period did quieten it, so this is not just a myth and was definitely used. Once again I have never encountered it myself but I know a man.......

In the 1930's one of Alf Baker's uncles had a 1928 Triumph. It was running well enough but he decided it needed a decoke. He had bought it from a patternmaker and on removing the barrel he found it had a wooden connecting rod. Incredible? Yes, but Alf swears it is true. Could an incredibly hard wood like Lignum Vitae have stood up to the comparatively modest pressures involved in one of those early engines?

Another uncle bought an early sidevalve Douglas which broke down on the way home. Removing the barrel he found the gudgeon pin had broken: Not surprising as it was made of wood! Not to be beaten he cut another one out of a hedgerow tree, fitted it and drove home! Another uncle.......I could go on!

248

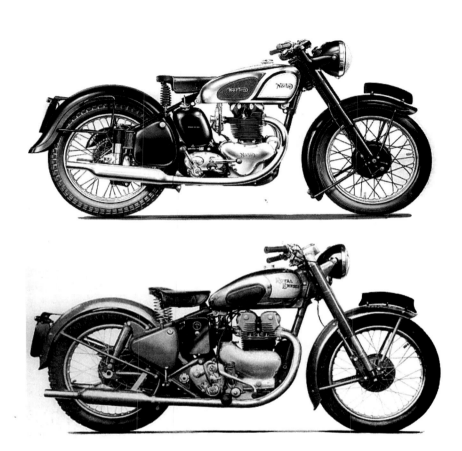

(Top) The 1949 500cc Norton Dominator Twin. Norton got it right first time and this basic engine design was to continue for years. A worthy challenger to all other twins of the period.
(Bottom) The 1949 500cc Royal Enfield twin. A beautifully proportioned machine and in many ways ahead of the opposition: Swinging arm rear suspension and alloy cylinder heads. Sales, however, always remained in the shadow of the leading makers.

(Top) Late 1920's Brough Superior. This is the 680cc machine. Jim Staff had the bigger model, the 1927 1,000cc SS 100. (Bottom) 1936 SS80 1,000cc sidevalve Brough Superior. For thirty years I had the pleasure of owning and restoring the actual 1936 model exhibited at the 1935 Motorcycle Show.

Chapter Thirty Seven
"The Customer is Always Right"

So said Gordon Selfridge, but he wasn't in the motorcycle business!

Dealing with customers was, in the main, a great pleasure, but there were difficult ones! A doctor once told me that 10% of his patients gave him 90% of his problems. That proportion, in my experience, was about right for motorcycle customers. Good guys, most of them, but that small percentage could, on occasion, make life difficult!

We did prepare machines carefully and if trouble was encountered we were there to help. A genuine customer with a genuine complaint was no trouble at all: The problem was put right and the rider was quickly on his way again.

So what kind of problems did we encounter? On occasions a customer would race into the shop wailing "Me gearbox has gone!". "Where has it gone to?" I would ask. Needless to say, it hadn't gone anywhere... his chain had broken!

A problem that was always difficult, or impossible, to solve was when the customer came in and said something like this: "The bike has a slight misfire but it only shows up between 58 and 60mph." A tough one, this!

An old timer who looked like Mr. Pastry was a frequent visitor to the shop. He was, indeed, a motorcyclist from way back though he never bought anything from us, not even a pint of oil. One day he came in and asked if he could borrow a "Thingummywotsit" needed to extract the valves from his son-in-law's unusual motorcycle.

251

I said that I would lend it to him, without charge, if he would look after it and return it as soon as possible. "Thank you very much" he said "Samways will lend me theirs but I thought I would let you have the business!".

Chris Harrison has a photograph of the workshop of Wall's garage, Melbourne and on the wall is a notice which says "The man that lends the tools is out collecting them". Not a bad slogan, echoing Bill Shakespeare's statement a few hundred years ago "Neither a borrower or a lender be."

On one occasion a none too pleasant customer pleaded with me to lend him a hacksaw as he couldn't afford to buy one. I lent him a hacksaw for a week but when it had not been returned five weeks later I went round to his house to collect it. He came to the door and with ill grace reluctantly handed it back, first taking out the blade! That was my blade he had broken or worn out: The one that he had bought was his!

Polish customers were marvellous: Hardly any problem customers in the Polish community. They arrived in England after the War with nothing but undeterred, they buckled down to often low paid jobs and worked as hard as they could. Their first objective was to buy a house and despite all difficulties they always achieved it. Having bought a house they would then permit themselves the luxury of a second-hand motorcycle.

Most of them had unpronounceable names and we would often abbreviate them to a shorter anglicised form which they invariably accepted with good grace! I remember one man in particular whose name we could not pronounce so we shortened it to Bocig, so to us he was always Billy Bocig. A diminutive chap with an impish smile who remained a customer for years.

One of the oddest Polish customers we had also had a long unpronounceable name. I have forgotten what it was, so let's call him "Woozynook". He came in with his sixteen year old son to buy a motorcycle. No trouble, the bike was fine, but a month or so later the Police came round to tell us that the son was being prosecuted as he was under sixteen years of age so he could not hold a driving licence or be insured.

I had completed the insurance proposal and got him to sign it in the presence of his father and the son's age had been declared as sixteen. I immediately went round to see the father and asked him what the devil he was doing, putting a false age on the insurance proposal form. "It was up to you to find out that my son was under sixteen" he replied! Well, there's nowt so queer as folk, as they say in Yorkshire and no doubt there is an equivalent saying in Warsaw!

But the oddest Polish customer of all was a man of about forty years old who bought a modestly priced 350 Matchless. Well, he said he was Polish and had the usual unpronounceable name. He spoke well with a slight accent which I presumed was Polish. He said he was a self-employed market gardener working on allotments near Normanton Recreation Ground.

We saw him from time to time when he called in at the shop. After about six months he went out to start his bike but collapsed and died of a heart attack.

The Police came to see us because he had *no identity at all.* He was in lodgings at the address he had given us and would go out in the morning to work on his allotment then return in the evening. *but there was no allotment.* He was not registered ill or unemployed and drew nothing from the State, so who was he and how did he earn a living?

A criminal? Surely not as he led a very frugal life. Drugs? Not on the scene in those days. A plant from a foreign power to find out what he could about Rolls Royce in Derby? Too fanciful to be believed.

So nothing of any kind was ever discovered about him and no identity was ever established: Whatever the true story was it went to the grave with the man with no name.

On one occasion we sold a motorcycle with unit construction engine and gearbox. The dipstick was attached to the oil filler-cap which was on the top of the crankcase. One day the customer hurtled into the shop, spluttering with rage. The engine was spurting oil all over the garage and he had never seen anything like it in his life: Something must be done immediately!

I went to see the bike and, sure enough, there was oil everywhere. Instead of filling the engine to dipstick level the customer had filled the whole engine/gearbox unit to the brim with oil so when the engine was started the oil did, indeed, fly everywhere!

Some customers flatteringly credited us with clairvoyant powers, such as "You knew that the dynamo/dipswitch/chain/ tyre would give trouble in three months time! Reserves of patience had to be drawn upon and the customer got out of trouble!

Call outs could be a problem as it is expensive to go out to see a machine with the necessary means to transport it back. Unavoidable in many cases, of course, but we were far too often called out to a "broken down" machine which had merely run out of petrol.

Once we were called out to a machine which had such a dreadful engine knock that the customer dared not ride it. When we got there we found that it did, indeed, kick up an enormous racket when started up but the noise was not from the engine but from the silencer.

On questioning the customer we found that he had rammed an iron bar down the silencer to "make it sound more sporty". The broken baffles were merely jangling in the silencer!

Running a machine completely out of oil until the engine seized was commonplace and, invariably our fault. It should not have used so much oil or needed the oil checking!

But when it came to customer complaints a fellow motorcycle dealer confessed to me that a powerfully built six-foot six-inch tall customer threatening to smash his brains out could be faced with equanimity but a four foot eight inch mother, incandescent with rage over her son's sick motorcycle scared the hell out of him!

A cross we had to bear in the motorcycle trade was the self appointed expert! Such experts would bring a machine along to you, explain what was wrong with it and tell you how to mend it. Their expertise, of course, always stopped short of being able to do the job themselves! Their diagnosis would invariably be entirely mistaken and their method of repair completely useless.

Another problem we often had to face was when a man had owned a machine for six months or more then came back to say that the engine/gearbox/magneto had packed up and motorcycle repairer X had told them that it would cost nine hundred pounds and four pence half penny to repair it, or some ridiculous sum. If the work had not been done we had the opportunity to carry it out as a sensible price, a fraction of the price quoted.

If, however, he had actually paid repairer X the ridiculous sum without consulting us and then expected us to refund the money this did put us in an impossible position. At such times saint-like patience was required... though sometimes impossible to achieve!

Another curse imposed by the self styled experts was when they came along with a pal who was interested in buying a machine. In this case the "expert" had to show his importance, in the eyes of his friend, by "crabbing" the sale. To approve the purchase would be no good: That would be accepting that the dealer knew what he was talking about!

But to condemn the sale had a twofold purpose: It would demonstrate his mastery of mechanics as far superior to that of the dealer and, in addition, put him completely in charge of the situation and show his pal what a clever chap he was. An aborted sale, therefore, was his ideal objective and in such circumstances it would be maddening to see a potential customer turned away from a perfectly sound machine that would have suited him very well indeed.

What has never ceased to amaze me is that the word of a qualified engineer with a vast range of experience and the welfare of his customer paramount because that is his bread and butter will invariably be completely ignored if the "Expert" pal says the opposite.

But all these problems were in the minority, confined to a tiny percentage of customers and for most of the time everything went well. The customer was supplied with a machine that suited his requirements that served him well. If trouble was encountered it was repaired either free of charge or at modest cost.

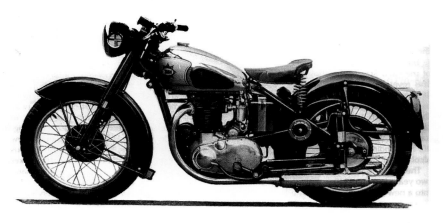

(Top) 1949 500cc B.S.A. Star Twin. The B.S.A. twins fought for supremacy with the Triumph twins. In 1949 this was B.S.A.'s answer to the Triumph Tiger 100, sports version of their A7. Higher compression engine and even twin carburettors, for 1949 only.

(Bottom) The 350cc E.M.C.. An unusual design. A two-stroke with the Puch type pair of cylinders and common combustion chamber. A massive machine for a 350 and though enjoyable to ride they were not famous for high performance. Like Scotts they were critical on oiling and could easily tighten up.

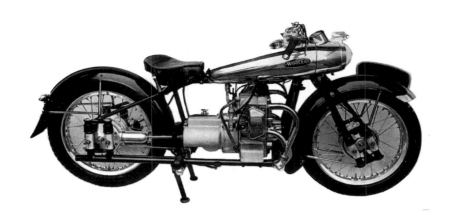

(Top) Wooler had made motorcycles in the early 1920's with the petrol tank protruding in front of the steering head, hence "The Flying Banana". Their post-war design still retained this feature, but with an imaginative 500cc flat four engine. Sadly it never went into production.
(Bottom) The 250 Panther was back after the war, but, unfortunately not at £29.17.6! Dowty forks were fitted in 1947.

SERVICE AT DERBY

Motor Cyclists Establish Successful Repair Business

TWENTY months ago Macton Motors, of 25, Melbourne Street, Derby, commenced business. The main object of the two partners, P. McManus and H. Tunaley, was to establish a first-class business in sales and service.

Both the partners are former members of the Rolls-Royce technical staff and they spent their spare time in two years before opening in preparing their workshop. They knocked down dividing walls and erected supporting girders before putting in windows and doors themselves, as well as relaying the floor surface. Refinements include power plugs for all the vises. Every repair is given a comprehensive workshop report, including details of all work carried out and material used.

The firm's showrooms are equally well planned and give a very favourable impression to passers-by.

THE EFFICIENT APPEARANCE of the Macton workshops is apparent in this photograph of one corner of the premises

Our writeup in The Motorcycle and Cycle Trader October 8th 1948.

Chapter Thirty Eight
Back on Track

From the time that petrol was restored in June 1948 we were pitched into a hectic time with so much to do. Business was starting to develop and, in addition, there were still trials and grass track races. I got engaged to Edna later in the year so the search was on to find somewhere to live. Accommodation was almost impossible to obtain as there was an enormous demand but I was fortunate enough to obtain the tenancy of a flat at 72 Wilson Street, over the Derby Boy Scout headquarters.

From then on it was all hands to the pumps to refurbish it completely. Fortunately all my friends willingly lent a hand.

Through the winter of 1948/49 I spent every weekend when I was not working on the flat riding over to Rhyl to see Edna. I would finish work at the shop at 5pm on Saturday night and start out for Rhyl. This, of course, meant riding in every kind of winter weather and with no time to get anything to eat before I started out so I would be cold and hungry when I arrived.

I would then stay in Rhyl all Sunday and start back for Derby early Monday morning to be back at work. This would mean a frantic rush to get machines sold on Saturday ready for off.

So 1948 came to an end and the New Year lay ahead: Surely an easier road than 1948 was in prospect, wasn't it?

As 1949 dawned, petrol was still rationed as, of course, was food. Tax for up to 150cc was 17s 6d, up to 250cc £1 17 6d, over 250cc £3 15s, and sidecars or three-wheelers £5.

Early in the year Nortons brought out the 500T trials model with all alloy barrel and head and Hugh Viney, A.J.S.. mounted, as usual won his third successive Scottish Six Days Trial.

In the T.T. the veteran rider, Harold Daniell, won the Senior on a Norton, Freddie Frith won the Junior on a Velocette for the second time in a row and Barrington on a Guzzi won the Lightweight. Tommy Wood, also Guzzi mounted, was second with the indomitable Roland Pike on his home tuned Pike Rudge storming home in third place.

In the Clubman's T.T., the 350 B.S.A. Gold Stars appeared for the first time and Harold Clarke won on one. In the Senior Clubman's, Geoff Duke commenced his brilliant road racing career by winning on a Norton, having graduated from trials, scrambles and, of course, "The impossible ascent" on the Clwydian Range!

Freddie Frith was to go on to win the 350 World Championship on his Works Velocette and for his contribution to the sport of motorcycling he became the first rider to be awarded a British Honour, the Order of the British Empire.

In the Manx Grand Prix in September Geoff Duke had his second Isle of Man win when he won the Senior Manx Grand Prix, only a fraction of a second outside the 1948 Senior T.T. winning speed of 86.928mph.

The great Triumph designer, Edward Turner, was always in touch with American thinking on motorcycle matters and his answer to their continual demand for "more cubes" was a bigger version of the Triumph twin, the 650cc Thunderbird. Three of the three new Thunderbirds were ridden from Coventry to Montlhery where they covered 500 miles, lapping in the nineties and ending with final laps of 100mph.

B.S.A., too, answered with their 650cc Golden Flash which was also destined to be a great success so the age of the "Superbike" had arrived.

Our marriage was arranged for May 1949 and a new 350 B.32 Competition B.S.A. was bought for the occasion. Price, if I remember rightly, £164 and a few shillings. The marriage date raced towards us with work at the flat redoubled to get it ready on time. This was finally accomplished by a whisker!

Getting married is a momentous milestone in anyone's life and, without doubt, the subject of endless witticisms. For example "I never knew what happiness was until I got married.....and then it was too late!" Or "There are no unhappy marriages..... the problem is living together afterwards!"

Another saying is one you should relate to a female audience with a suitably solemn demeanour "I know that we tease you ladies and make fun of you, but the longer I live the more convinced I am that behind every successful man......" you now pause to enable your audience to assume a suitably simpering expression "stands an astonished mother in law!"

Not, I hasten to add, that this applied to me as I was always on the very best of terms with Edna's mother.

Finally a statement made by Marcus Aurelius nearly two thousand years ago but just as true today: "Marriage is a lottery". I have been very fortunate but no matter how carefully you may chose it is still a gamble and things can go wrong. Peter Ustinof tells of seeing an absolutely marvellous girl on a magazine cover. He went out of his way to arrange a meeting and married her. Later he was to divorce her and it cost him every penny he had. "It was a bargain", he said.

Our wedding was, of course, at Rhyl and the reception at Stella Maris where my mother put on a magnificent buffet wedding breakfast. All my motorcycling friends came over to stay at Stella Maris welcomed, as always, by my mother.

So a glorious Spring day, a new motorcycle and with a new bride on the pillion we headed for Llandridod Wells where we were to spend the night at the big hotel there. Confetti had been stuffed down the back of my shirt by the bagful and Edna had received the same treatment so we stopped on a river bank to attempt to get rid of it, but with limited success!

Next morning the run to Newquay where we were to spend our honeymoon. During the honeymoon we were getting off the B.S.A. when a old timer came across to me and said "If that was my motorcycle and that was my wife I would think I had the whole world in my hand". He was right, of course. The time went all too quickly and then it was back to Derby to start a new life on our wage from Macton Motors of £5 a week.

There is a theory that men marry girls like their mothers and although none of us ever realise that this could happen there is often a lot of truth in it. Edna was by no means a younger replica of my mother but they were similar in many ways. Edna, just like my mother, took to business like a duck to water and pitched in right away.

The summer of 1949 was hot and Edna found the heat in town dreadfully oppressive. At Rhyl, no matter how hot it is, there is always a sea breeze so it is always bearable, but there are no sea breezes in Derby! She soldiered on and did her best but it was hard going!

The workshop at 25 Melbourne Street was a vital part of our business, creating a refurbished flow of machines for us to sell. We had told Miss Currie that if she ever considered selling we would be interested in buying it. We had not been married many months, however, when we received a latter from Richardson and Linnell, the Estate Agents, notifying us that the premises were going up for auction.

In those days there was no protection of tenancy for business people: If you were on a weekly tenancy, as we were, all the landlord had to was to give you a week's notice and you were out at the end of the week.

Miss Currie, to our amazement, was getting married and leaving Derby. We went to see her but she refused to see us or speak to us. It was clear that if we were to hope to stay there our only chance was to turn up at the auction and bid. Whatever the premises were worth it was due to our cash and years of hard work but we were to get no allowance for any of that.

We did our homework and it appeared that the premises would realise £400/450. To have a reasonable margin we decided to go to £500. Don't laugh at these figures: To bring them in line with today's values you would have to multiply them seventy times or more!

The problem was that we were clearly, from an estate agent's point of view, the most likely buyers and the buyers who would pay the highest price. The auctioneer knew us so how could we avoid being run up?

We worked out a simple plan: A good customer of ours was Sydney Clarke, a bright young man with an excellent business head. T, Edna and I would sit together and bid up to £450. At that point, if the property had not been knocked down to us, we would get up and walk out, showing the auctioneer that his best prospect had gone. Sydney, in another part of the room, would then continue to bid up to our limit of £500.

Plan agreed, now all we had to do was to raise the money, or most of it. We banked with Martins Bank in the Market Place Derby and our Bank Manager, Mr. Gordon, was one of the "Old School". Lending restrictions were in force and he always took great pleasure in telling you that if someone came in to buy a car he could not lend them the money.

We did *not* want to buy a car but business property: Bricks and mortar as loved by Banks! We put our proposition to Mr. Gordon but had no chance! No way was he going to lend a shilling to brash young people like us! We were out on our collective ears!

Derbyshire Building Society really lent to house buyers but they were kind enough to agree to lend us the money and I have always been grateful to them.

So the day of the auction arrived. We continued bidding up to £450 and walked out as planned. We peered in a few minutes later to find that the premises had been knocked down to Sydney for £500.

We were, of course, absolutely delighted: We had secured the premises, business could continue unchanged and we had a measure of security. The premises were to be paid up in full within two years: Mr. Gordon need not have worried after all!

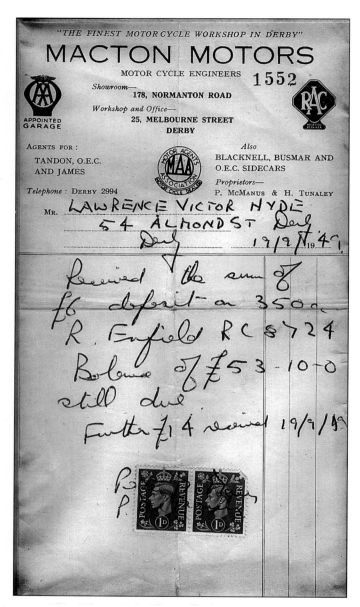

MR. *LAWRENCE VICTOR HYDE*
54 ALMOND ST Derby
Derby 19/9/19 *49*

Received the sum of
£6 deposit on 350 cc
R. Enfield RC 8724
Balance of £53-10-0
still due
Further £1 4 received 19/9/49

Ps
P.

Copy of a Macton Motors receipt dated 19/9/1949. Judging by the price paid this must have been an ex-WD 350 cc Royal Enfield.

264

(Top) The first post war B.S.A. Gold Star. This is the 1949 350cc B32 GS with all alloy engine, B.S.A. telescopic forks and plunger rear suspension. B.S.A. had their eye on the Clubman's T.T. with these machines and they were eventually to prove unbeatable. (Bottom) 1949 650cc Triumph Thunderbird. Superlative machines and a reliable upgrade from the five hundreds. The era of the superbike had arrived.

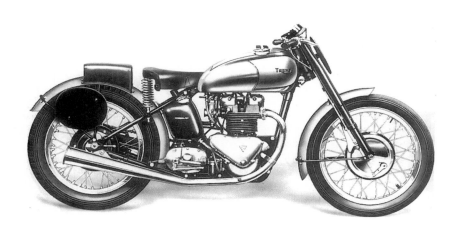

(Top) 1948 Triumph 500cc Grand Prix racer. Competitive with the Manx Norton, but without its reliability. Same basic engine design as the 1949 TR5 Trophy.

(Bottom) 1947 Triumph 350cc 3T Twin. Delightful to ride, but without the sparkling performance of the pre-war Tiger 80 single.

Chapter Thirty Nine
The End of the Nineteen Forties

1949 was an enormously important year for us with so much happening. Business was getting into top gear, Edna and I had got married, we had managed to buy 25 Melbourne Street and there were not enough hours in the day to cope with all we had to do.

T decided to have a crack at road racing and entered his Triumph Trophy at the Cadwell Park racing circuit. It was not specially tuned for the attempt, nor were higher compression pistons fitted, but T did carefully prepare it. He rode it to Cadwell and we went on one of the unusual 350cc E.M.C. motorcycles. They were twin-cylinder with a common combustion chamber, rather like the Puch design.

At the start of T's heat he shot into the lead and stayed there to win: A remarkable achievement against Manx Nortons and 7R A.J.S. racers. He did not win the final but he was not disgraced.

The International Six Days Trial was held in Wales that year so Edna and I went over on our B.32 B.S.A. to watch. Thoroughly enjoyable with so many unusual foreign machines to see, all new to us. The Army had also entered some of the new side-valve twins, specially designed for the services, a surprise to the motorcycle world as Triumph twins had always been overhead valve. We were impressed by their very quiet exhaust note. Murray Walker, riding one of the new 500T Trials Nortons, won a gold medal.

During the summer of 1949 Edna and I would often ride over to Rhyl, starting as I used to do at 5pm on a Saturday night and returning on the Monday morning. The time taken was amazingly consistent, only varying by a few minutes from the standard two hours 35 minutes. Summer holiday was spent at Rhyl and in November we were off on our motorcycle to stay at the Cumberland Hotel, London for the Motorcycle Show.

This was the first of our many visits together to the Motorcycle Show, always staying at the Cumberland Hotel. They were always enormously enjoyable and we filled every minute and of course, saw the Show which was, for us, of absorbing interest. There was much to see including the new breed of superbikes, the 650 Triumph Thunderbirds and the 650 B.S.A. Golden Flashes and one of the smaller, but no less interesting models, was the new 250cc Excelsior Talisman Twin with plunger rear suspension. A curiosity was the new Vespa scooter, seen by us for the first time: Would they ever catch on?

We discovered Soho, ate at a variety of restaurants, enjoyed the theatres, did all our Christmas shopping and luxuriated at the Cumberland Hotel. The bike was parked and we went everywhere by taxi which was not expensive in those days.

So the end of the year arrived with a marvellous Christmas at Stella Maris to finish it off. The 1940's were behind us, one of the most dramatic decades of the century and, without doubt, the most momentous of our lifetime to date. As the decade ended the effects of War were far from over. Petrol, clothing, food and confectionery were all rationed but the good news was that from December 4th the tea ration was to be increased to two and a half ounces a week! So things were looking up and Edna and I would be allowed to buy just over a quarter of a pound of tea per week between us! Black marketeers, however, seemed to manage to obtain goods in short supply to sell at inflated prices. Although we had to suffer petrol rationing, Norway, Belgium, France, Holland, Italy and Russia did not and even Germany signalled its intention to end petrol rationing early in the New Year.

Britain, however, was the world's largest motorcycle manufacturer. Ahead of us lay the 1950's and the prospects looked good! It was an exciting time to be in the world of motorcycles with new designs coming onto the market. Most leading manufacturers had unveiled their new vertical twins offering new dimensions of riding experience. Business was going well, I had my wife at my side and we eagerly looked forward to the next decade, ready to face any challenge.

(Top) The Nortons and Velocettes had battled for decades on the world's racing circuits, but now their era was drawing to a close. This was one of the last of the immortal KTT Velocettes. (Bottom) 1949 Manx Norton. The Velocette's worthy adversary.

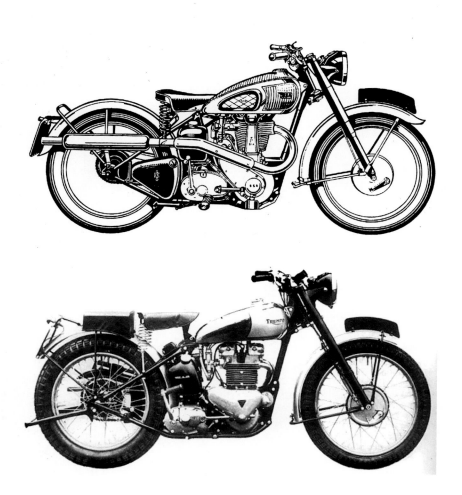

(Top) B.S.A. 350cc B32 Trials machine, This is a 1947 model,
very similar to our 1949 "Honeymoon express"!
(Bottom) 1949 500cc Triumph Trophy. Surely the last of the great
all rounders.(Ride it to and from work!) Trials and scrambles at the
weekends and even road racing at Cadwell Park. A magnificent
machine and just as much fun to ride fifty years on.

"Let us, then, be up and doing
With a heart for any fate"

Longfellow

271